HAL•LEONARD UKULELE PLAY-ALONG

Lennon & McCartney

AUDIO ACCESS INCLUDED

To access audio visit:
www.halleonard.com/mylibrary

Enter Code
7516-3018-6309-6922

ISBN 978-1-4234-9618-2

HAL•LEONARD®
7777 W. BLUEMOUND RD. P.O. BOX 13819 MILWAUKEE, WI 53213

For all works contained herein:
Unauthorized copying, arranging, adapting, recording, Internet posting, public performance, or other distribution of the printed or recorded music in this publication is an infringement of copyright.
Infringers are liable under the law.

Visit Hal Leonard Online at
www.halleonard.com

Hal•Leonard Ukulele Play-Along
Lennon & McCartney
VOL. 6

Audio Access Included

CONTENTS

Page	Title
4	And I Love Her
7	Day Tripper
10	Here, There and Everywhere
16	Hey Jude
20	Let It Be
13	Norwegian Wood (This Bird Has Flown)
26	Nowhere Man
24	Yesterday

And I Love Her

TRACK 1

Words and Music by John Lennon and Paul McCartney

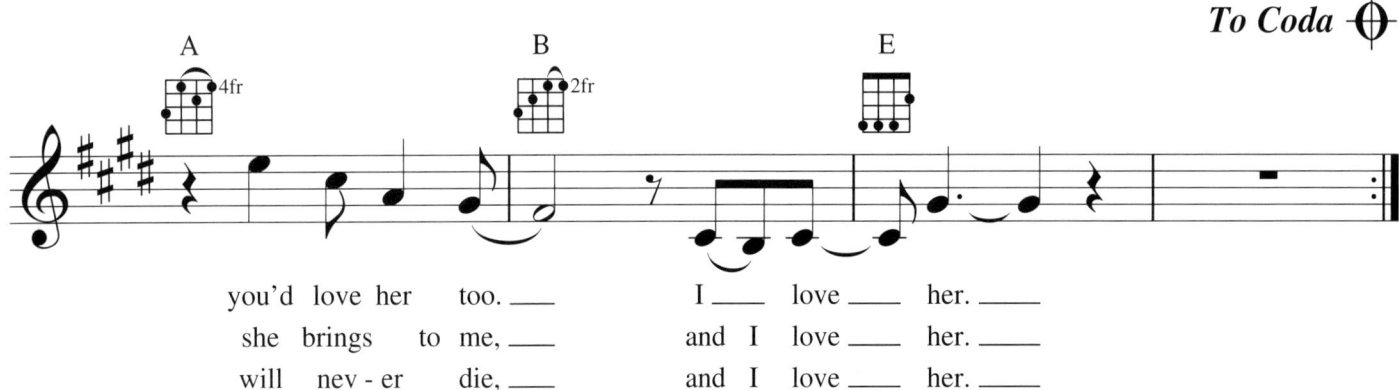

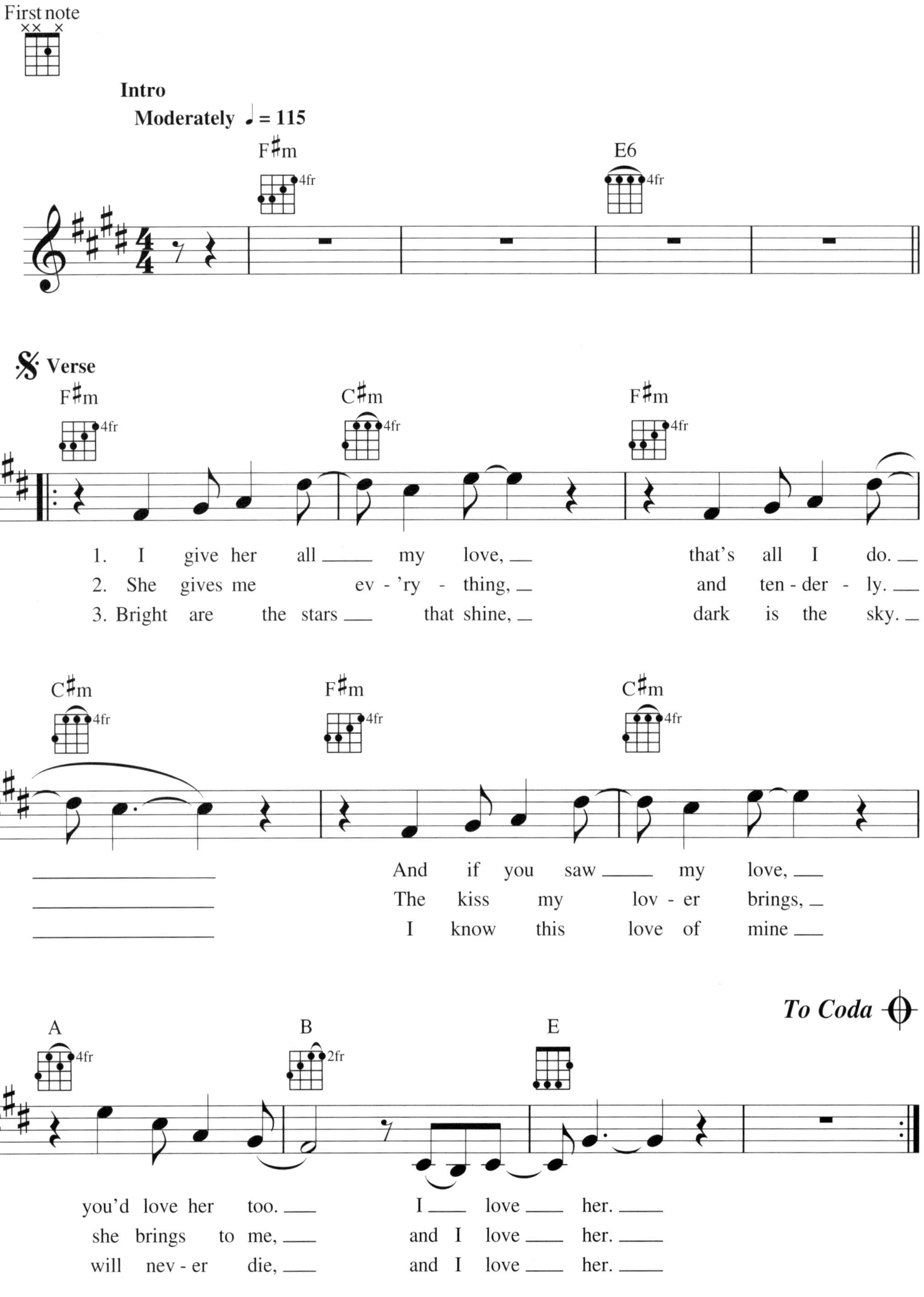

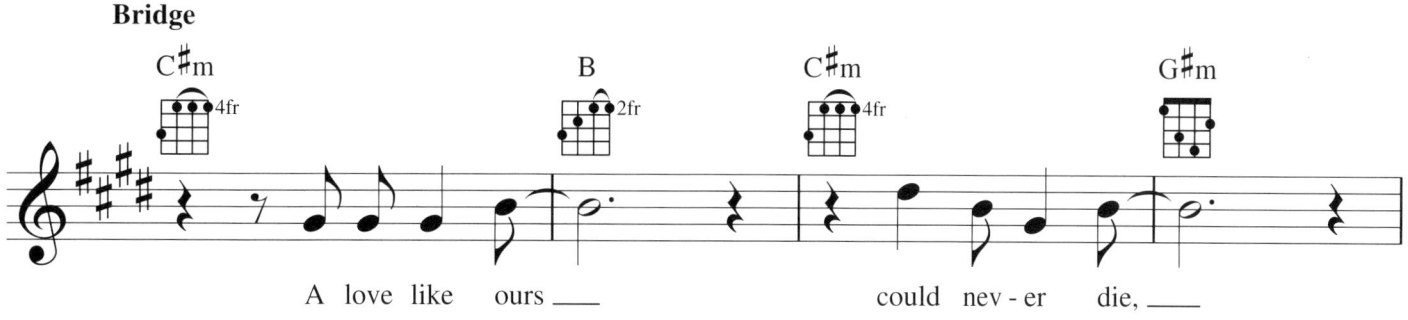
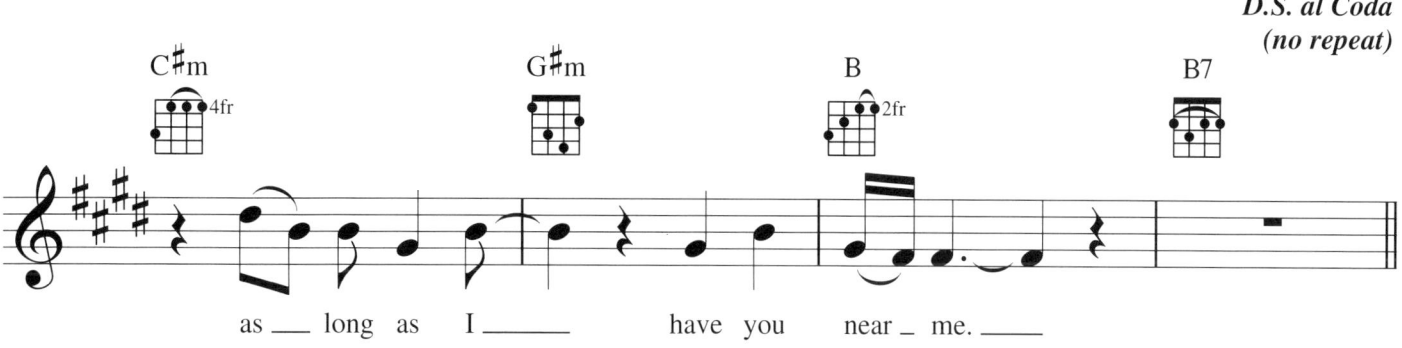

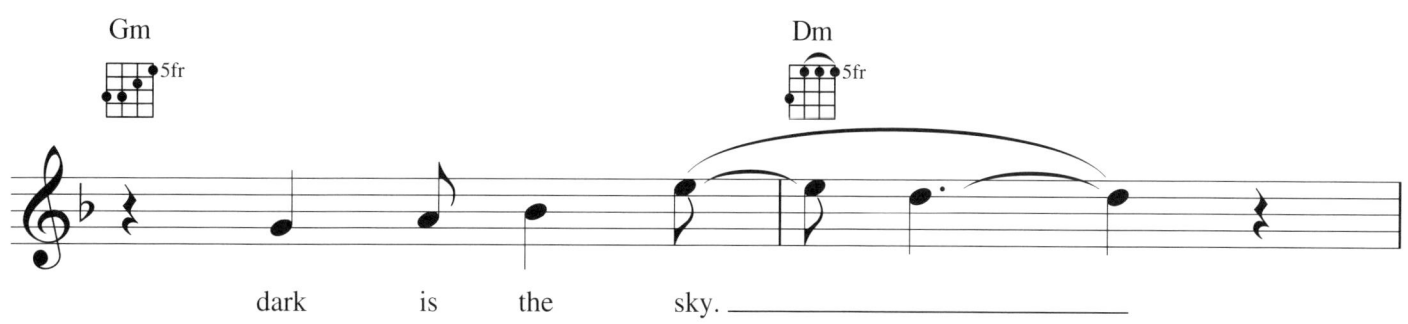
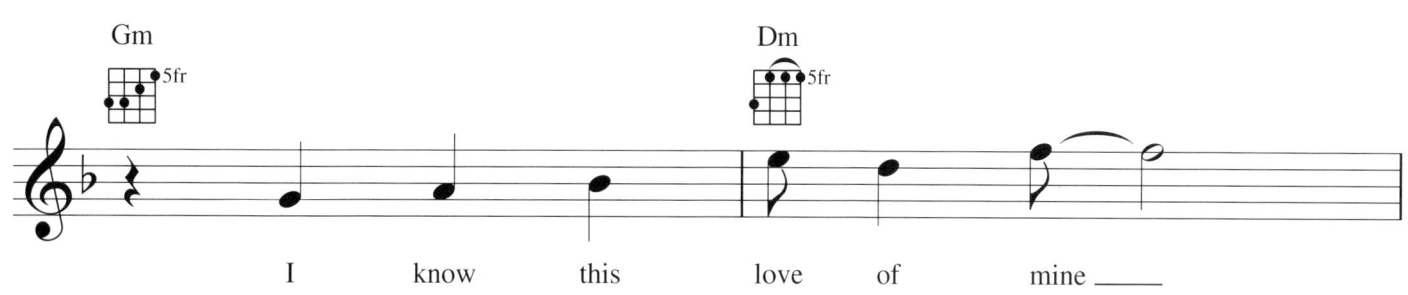

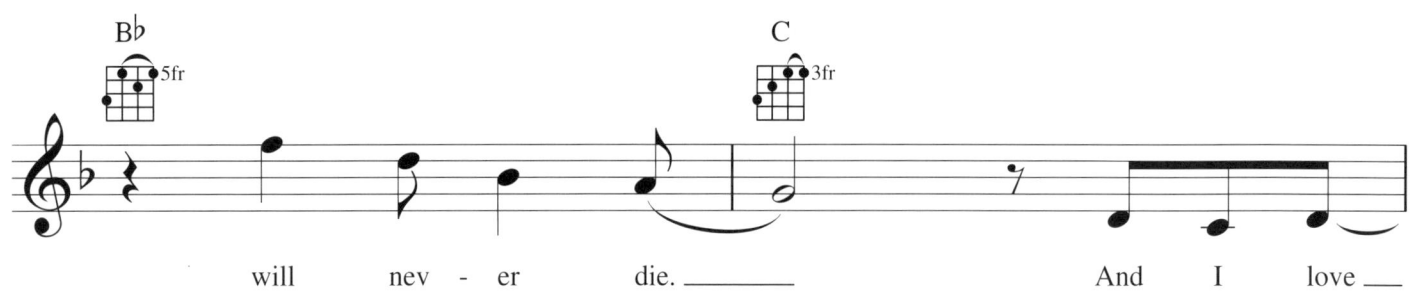
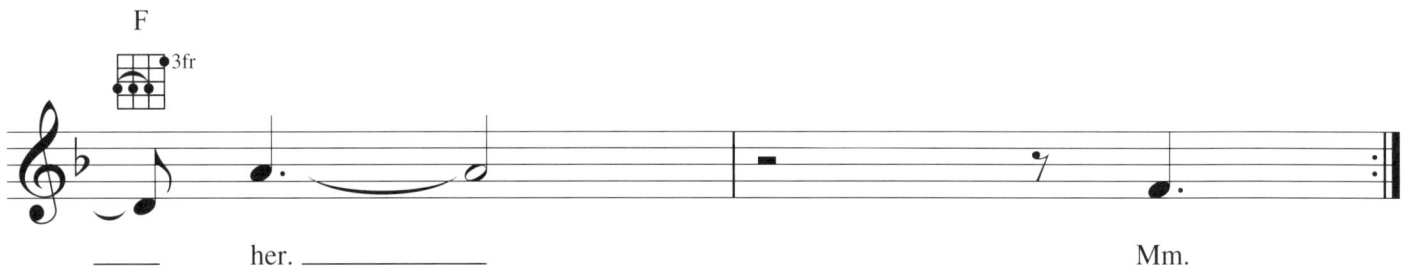

Outro

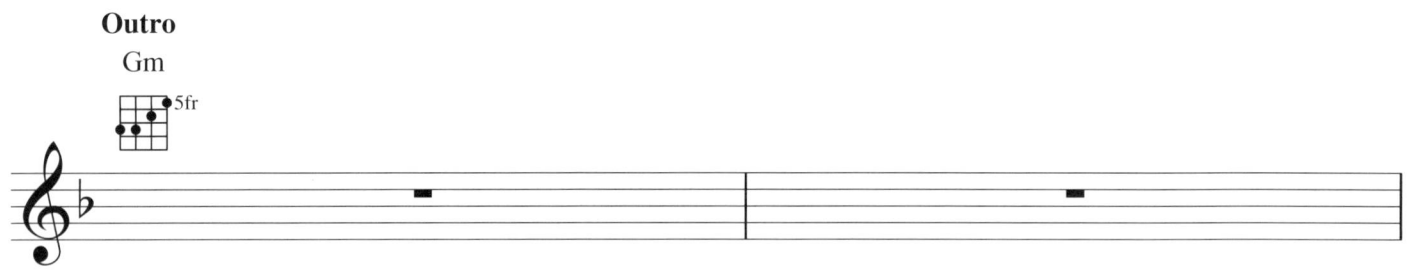
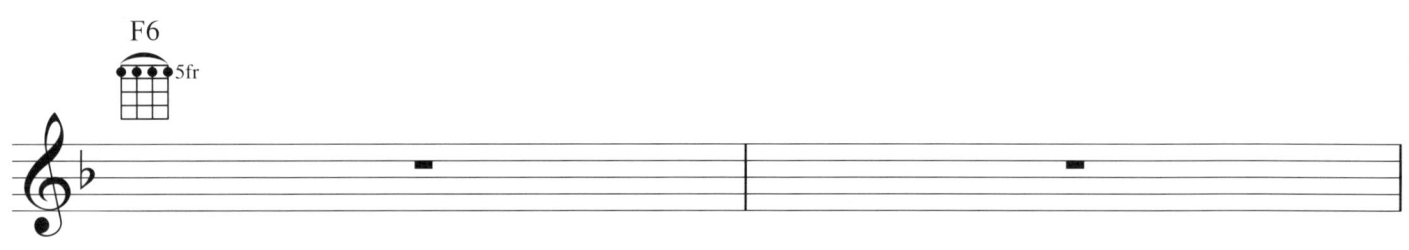
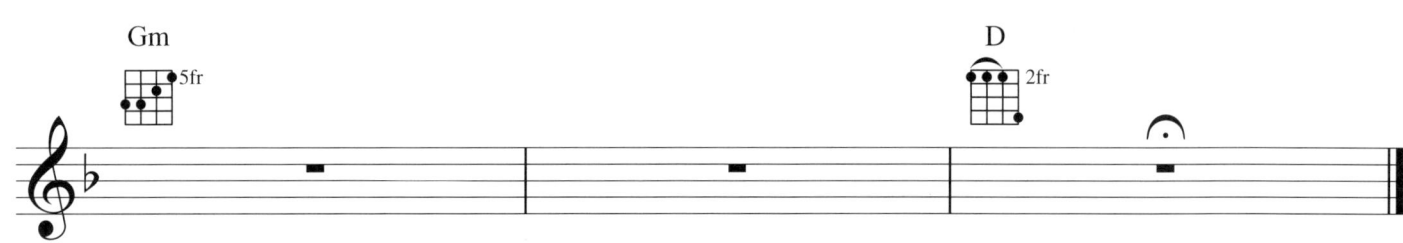

Day Tripper

Words and Music by John Lennon and Paul McCartney

TRACK 3

First note

Intro
Moderate Rock ♩ = 136

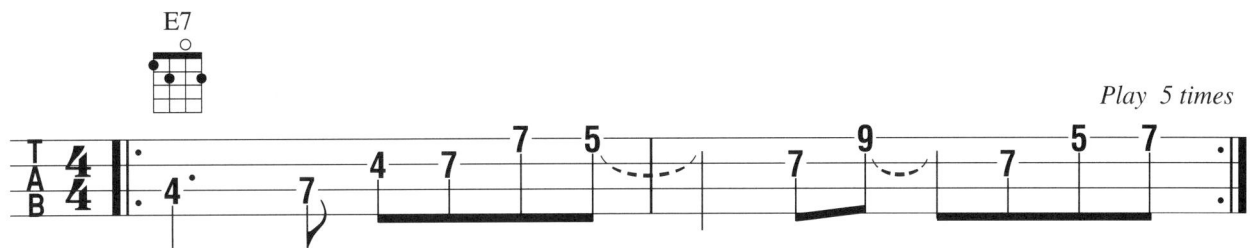

Play 5 times

Verse

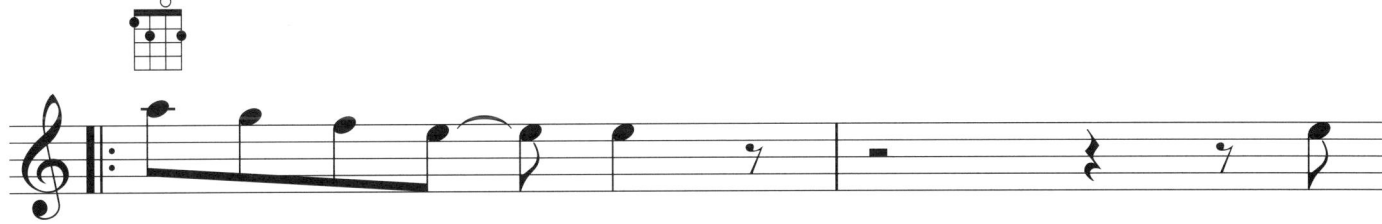

1. Got a good rea-son for tak-ing the eas-y way out.
2. She's a big teas-er, she took me half the way there.
3. Tried to please her, she on-ly played one night stands.

Got a good rea-son for
She's a big teas-er,
Tried to please her,

Copyright © 1965 Sony/ATV Music Publishing LLC
Copyright Renewed
All Rights Administered by Sony/ATV Music Publishing LLC, 8 Music Square West, Nashville, TN 37203
International Copyright Secured All Rights Reserved

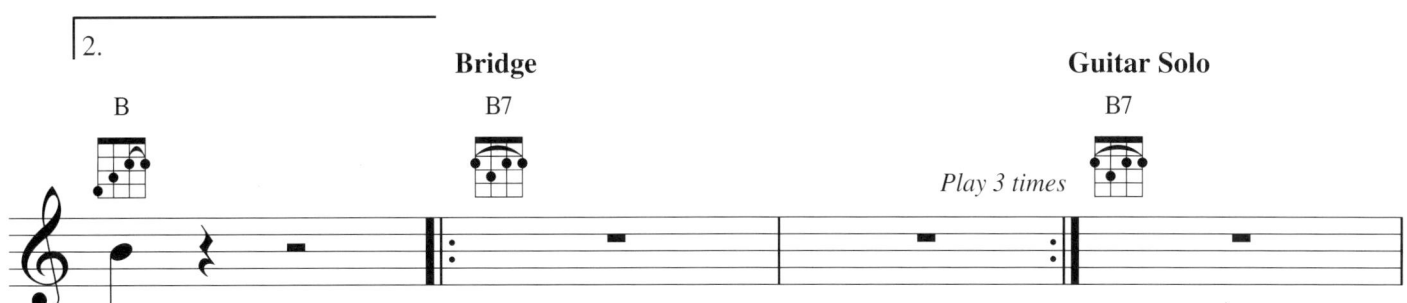

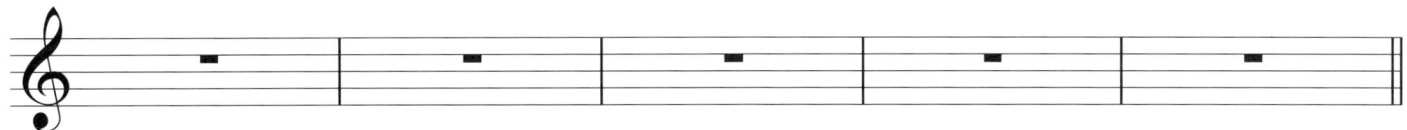

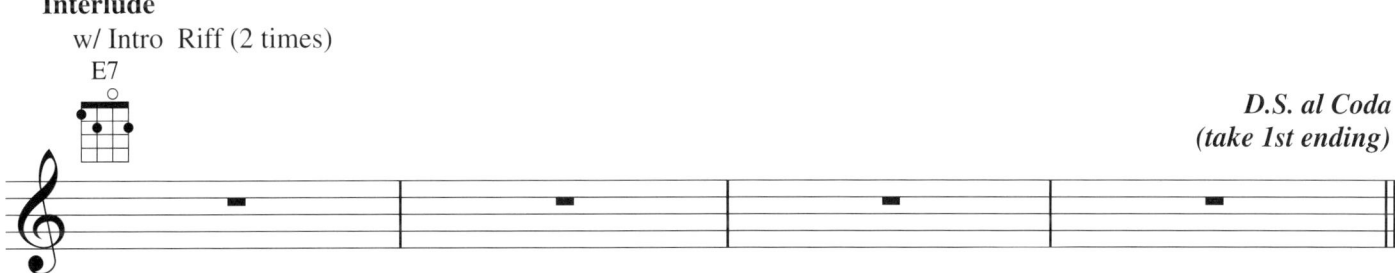

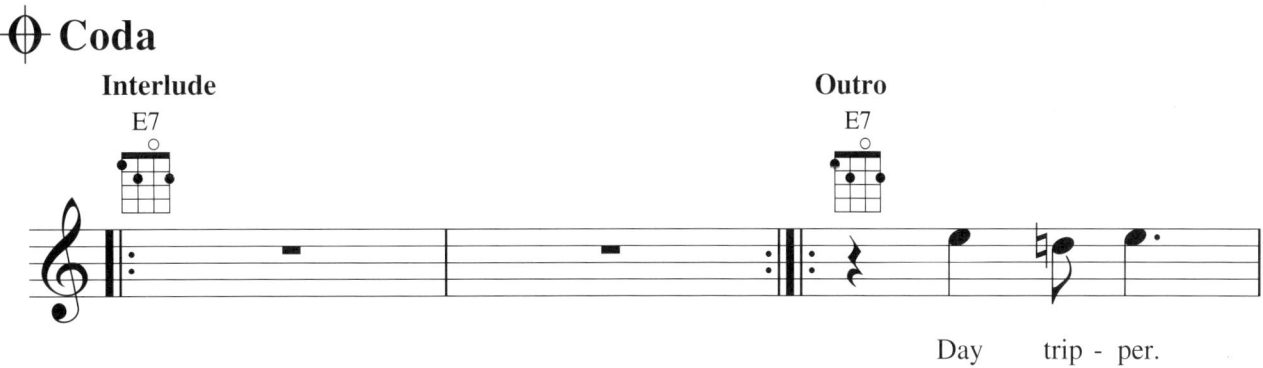

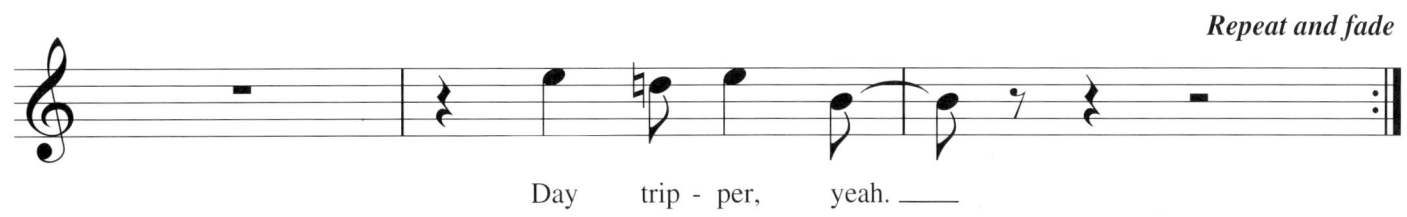

Here, There and Everywhere

Words and Music by John Lennon and Paul McCartney

To lead a bet-ter life, I need my love to be here.

1. Here, mak-ing each day of the year,
2. There, run-ning my hands through her hair,

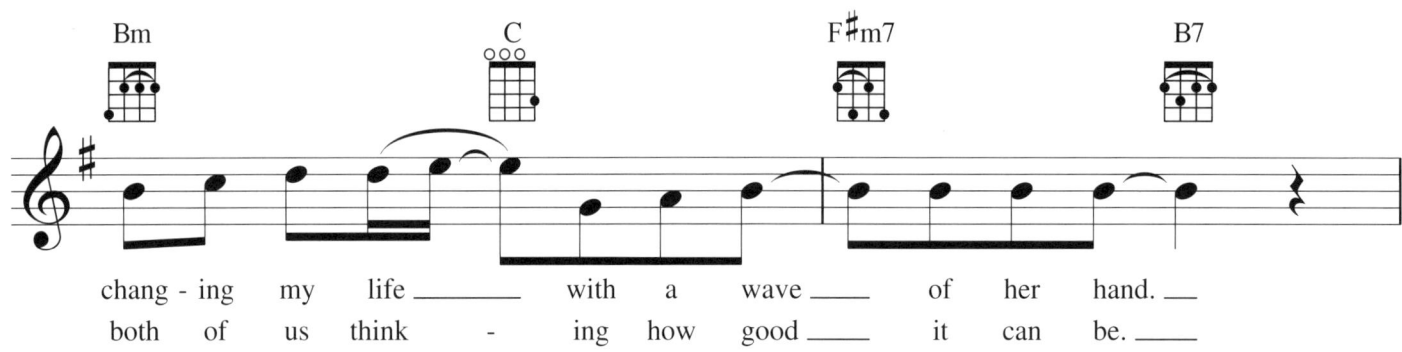

chang-ing my life with a wave of her hand.
both of us think-ing how good it can be.

No-bod-y can de-ny that there's some-thing there.
Some-one is speak-ing, but she does-n't know he's there.

Copyright © 1966 Sony/ATV Music Publishing LLC
Copyright Renewed
All Rights Administered by Sony/ATV Music Publishing LLC, 8 Music Square West, Nashville, TN 37203
International Copyright Secured   All Rights Reserved

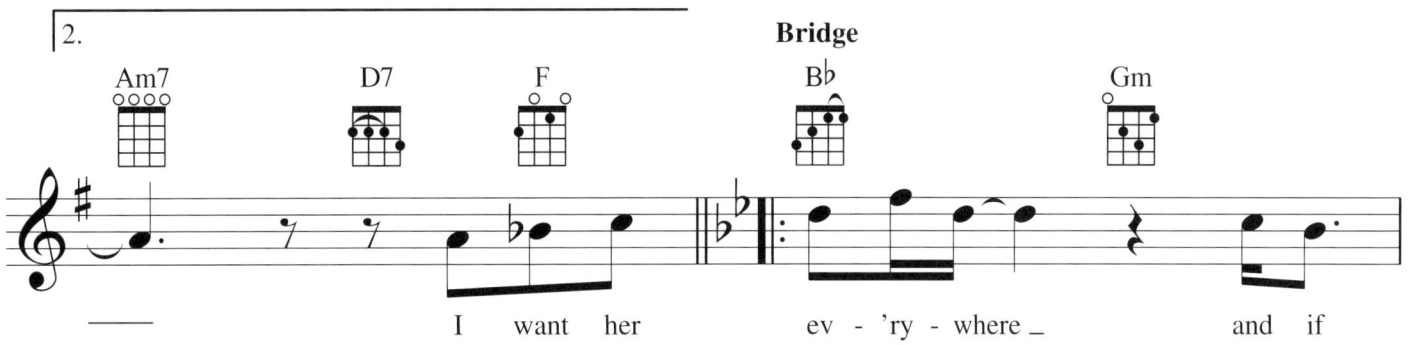
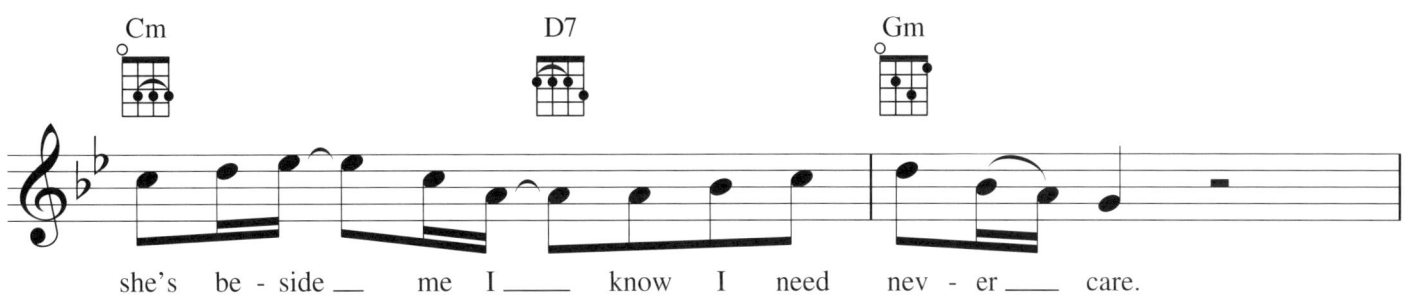

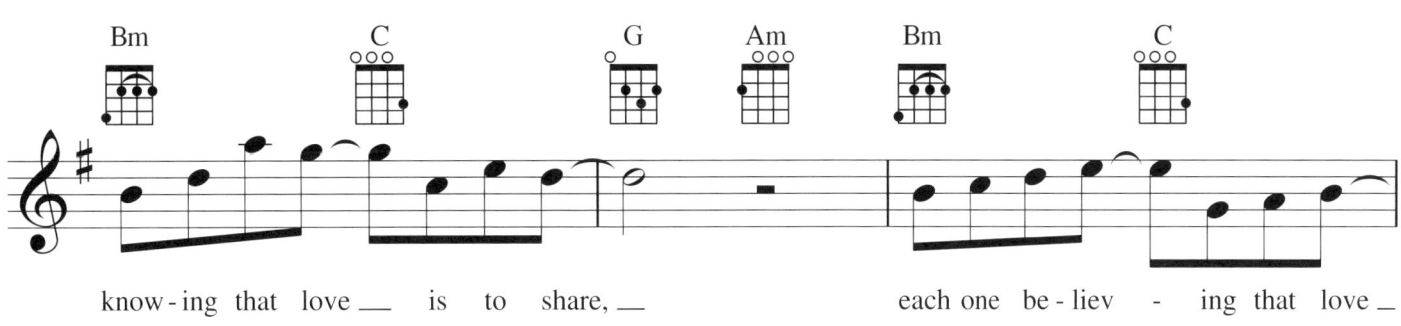
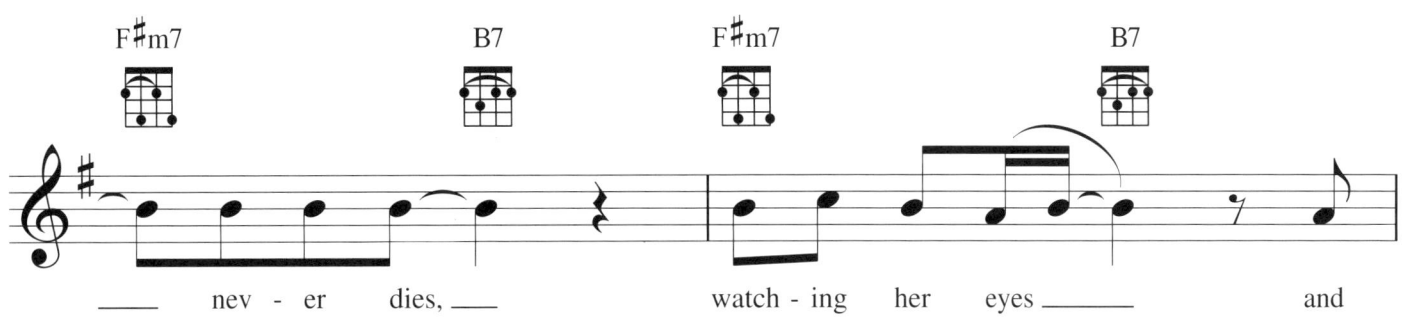

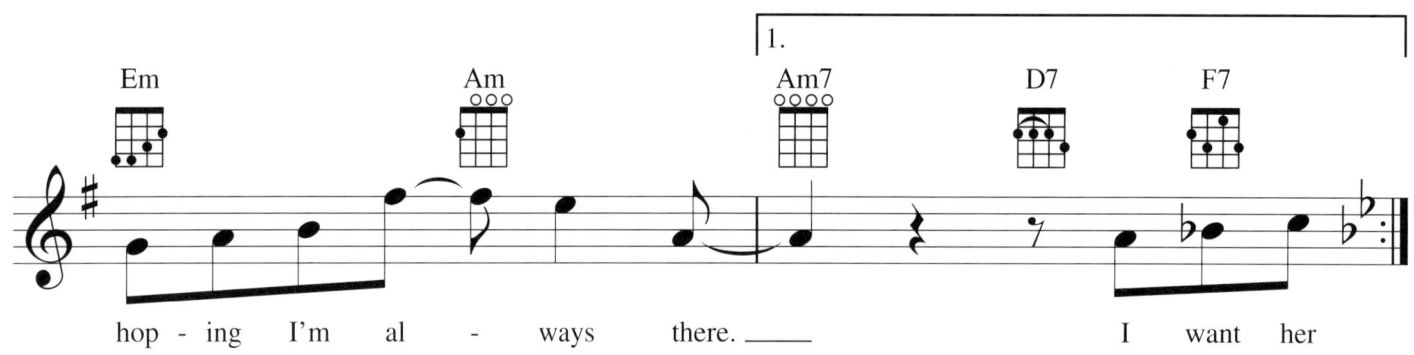

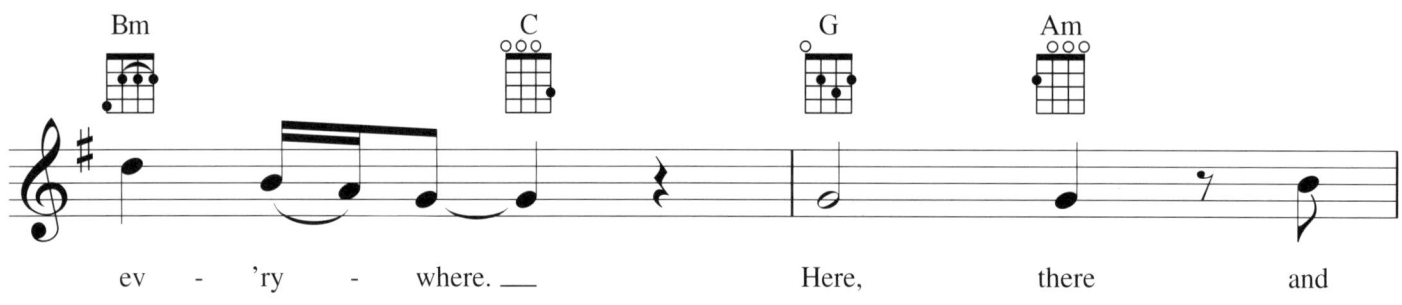
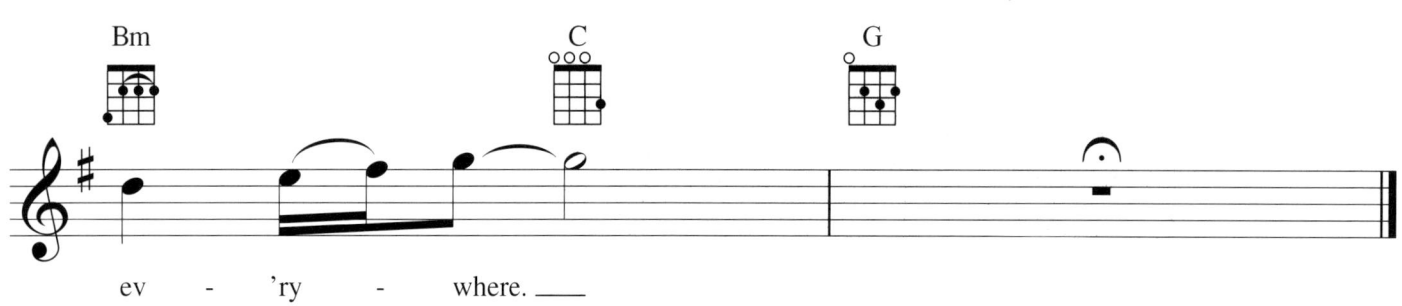

Norwegian Wood
(This Bird Has Flown)

Words and Music by John Lennon and Paul McCartney

First note

Intro
Moderately ♩ = 96

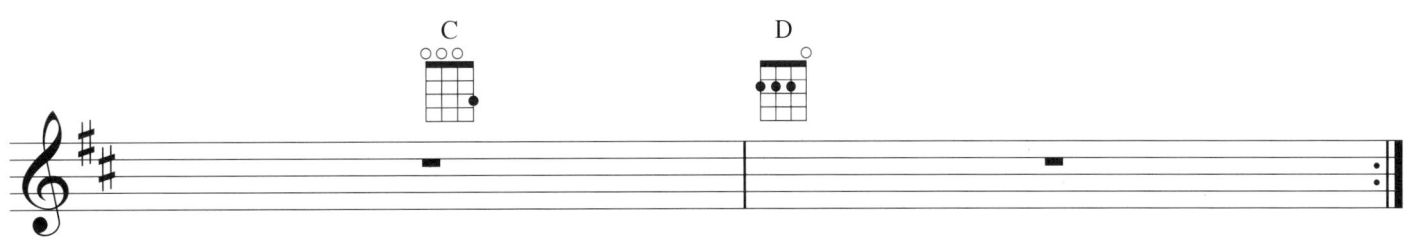

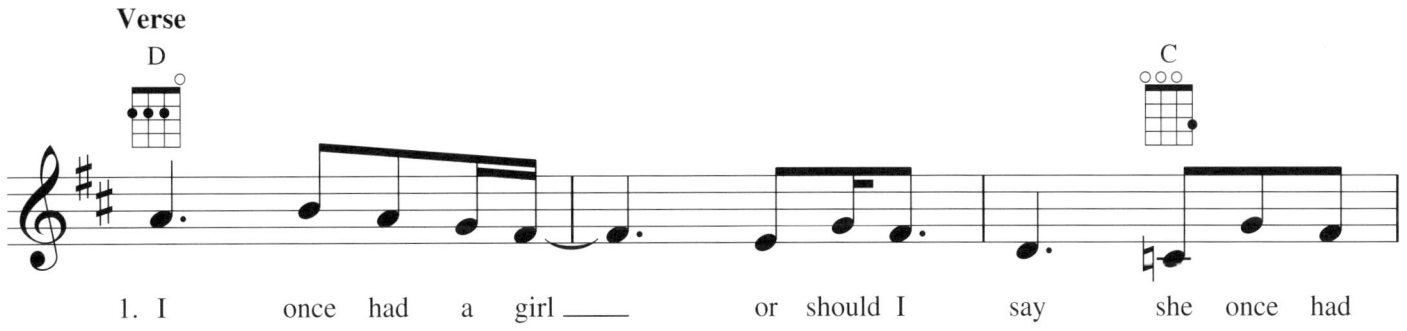

1. I once had a girl ___ or should I say she once had

me. She showed me her room, is-n't it

Copyright © 1965 Sony/ATV Music Publishing LLC
Copyright Renewed
All Rights Administered by Sony/ATV Music Publishing LLC, 8 Music Square West, Nashville, TN 37203
International Copyright Secured All Rights Reserved

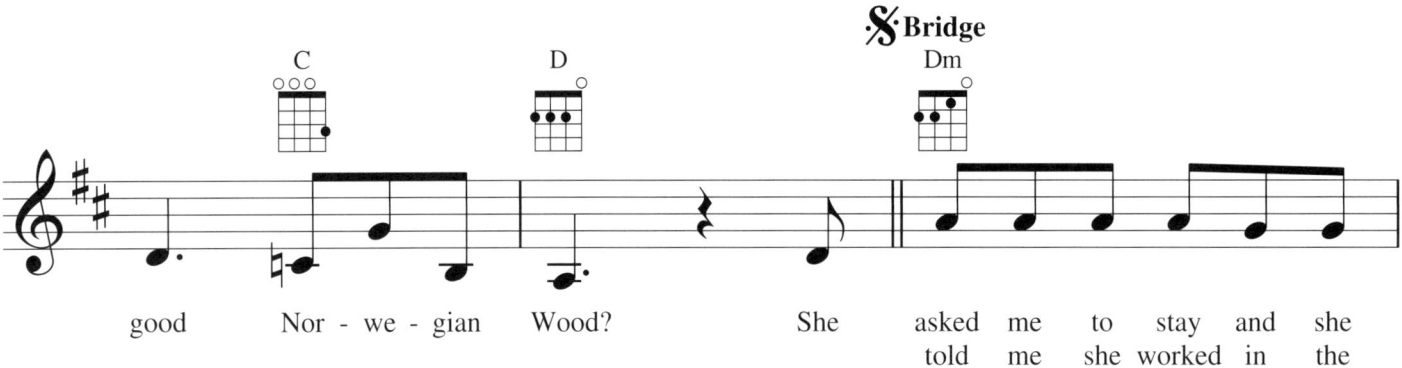

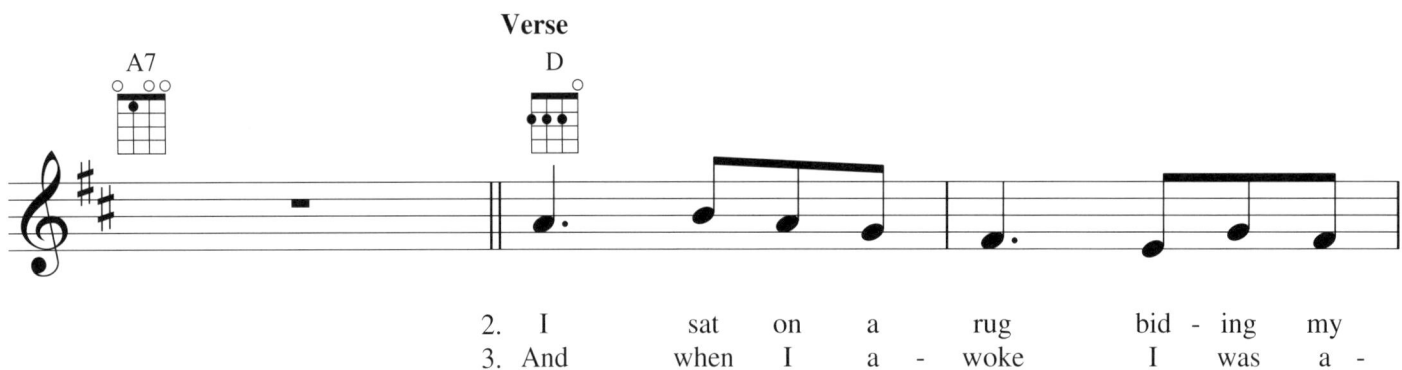
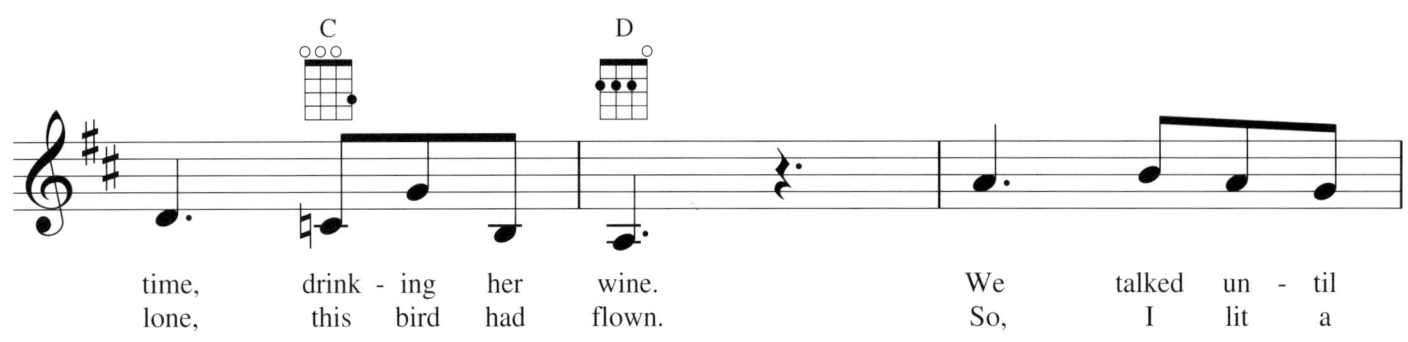

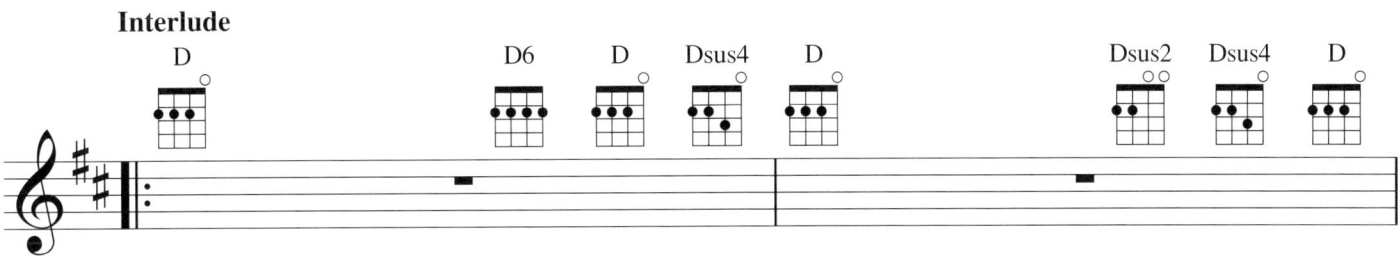
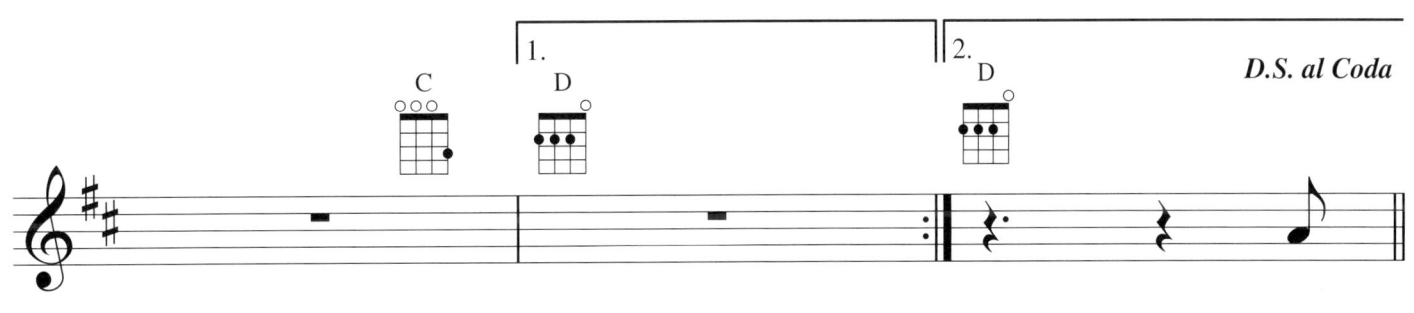
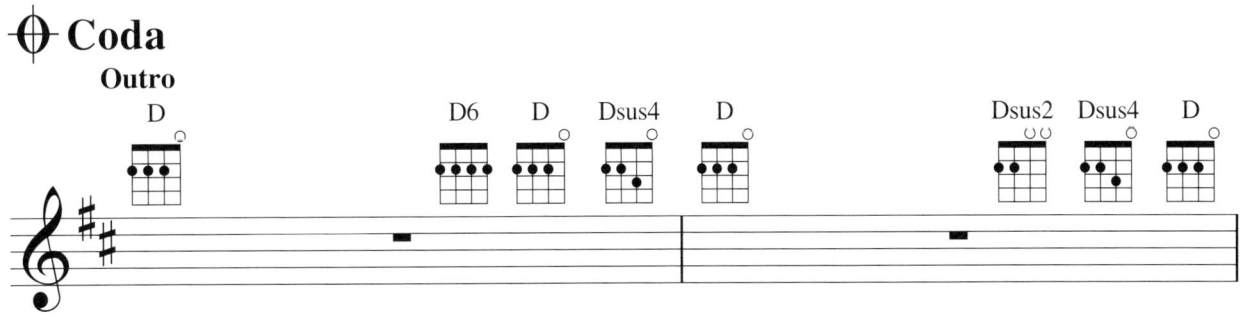
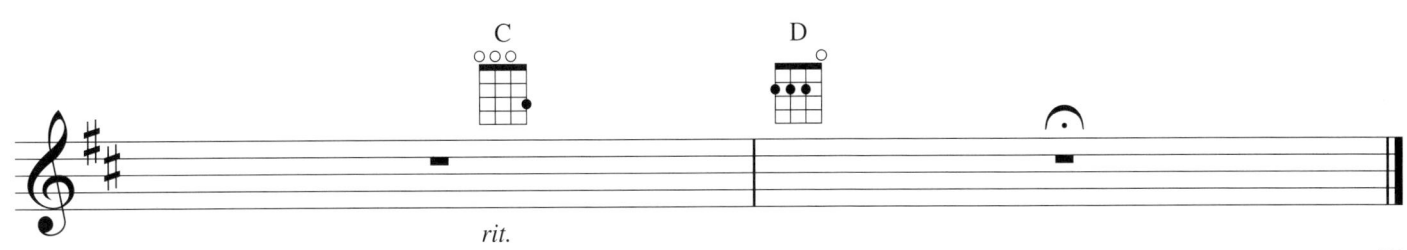

15

Hey Jude

Words and Music by John Lennon and Paul McCartney

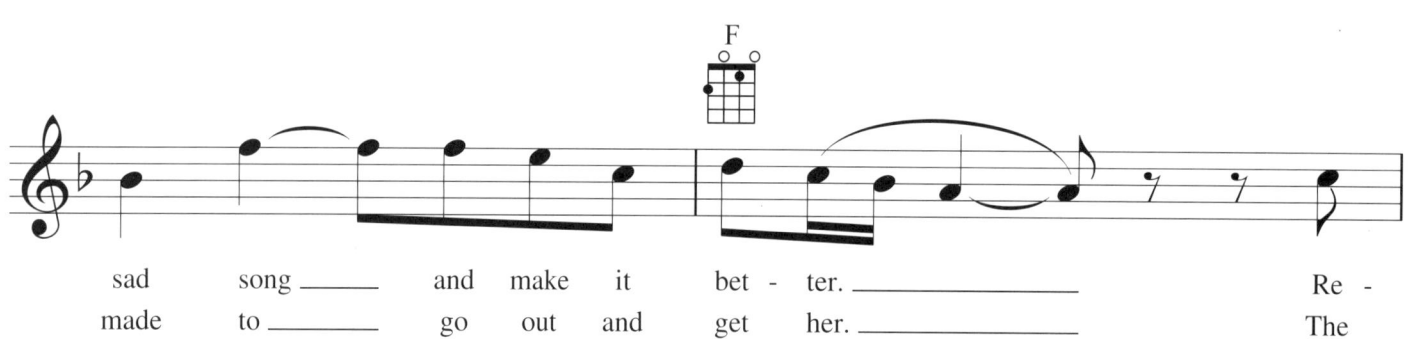

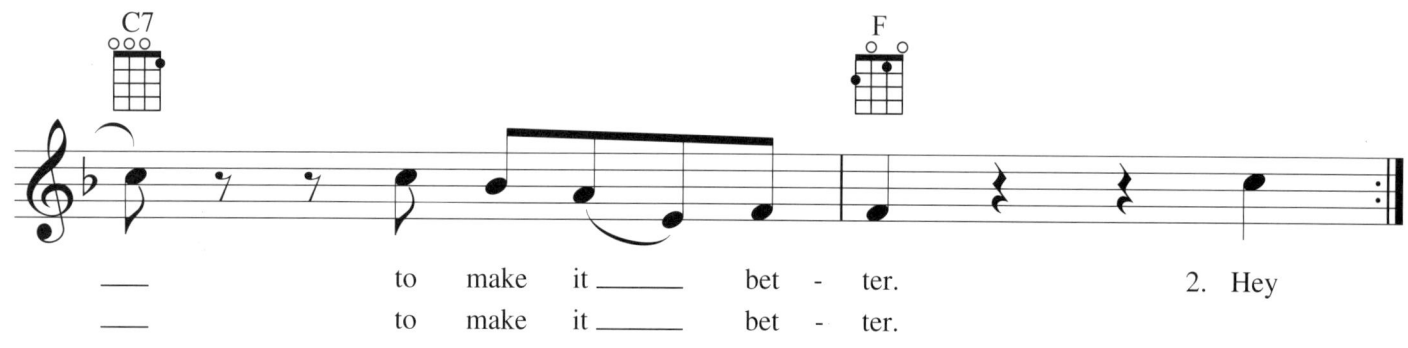

Copyright © 1968 Sony/ATV Music Publishing LLC
Copyright Renewed
All Rights Administered by Sony/ATV Music Publishing LLC, 8 Music Square West, Nashville, TN 37203
International Copyright Secured   All Rights Reserved

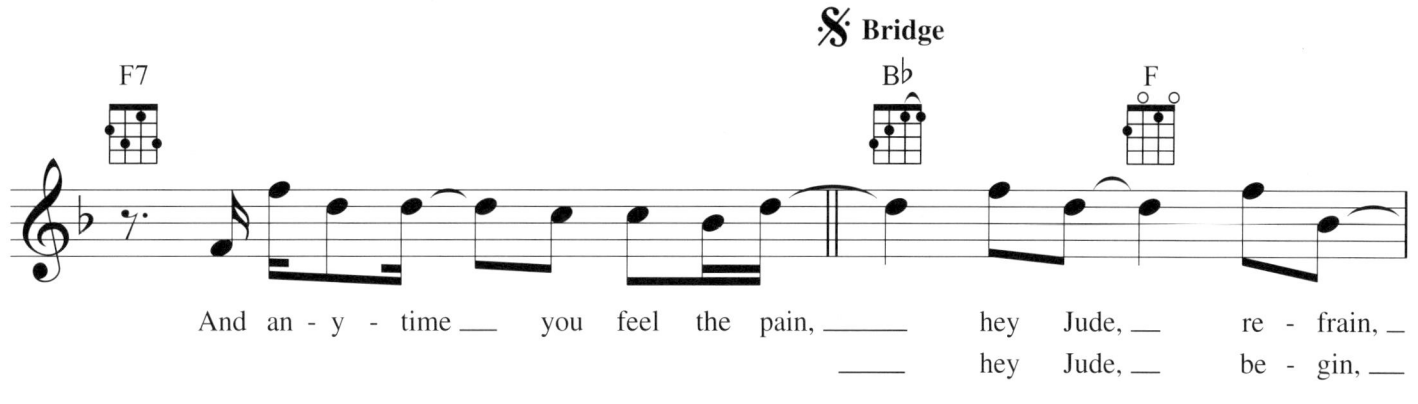
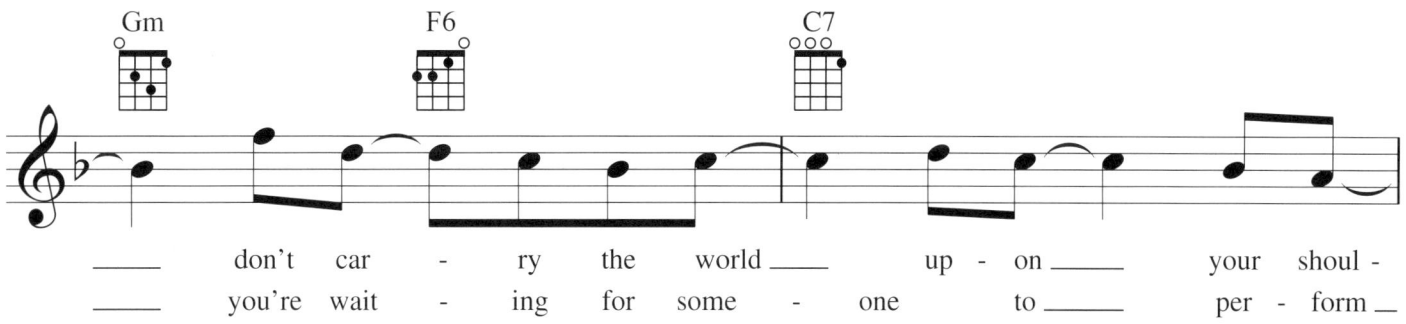

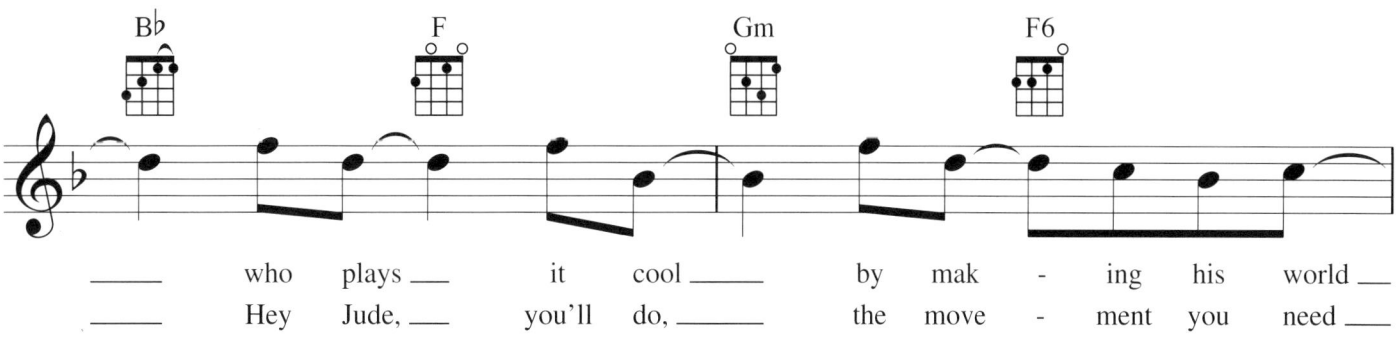
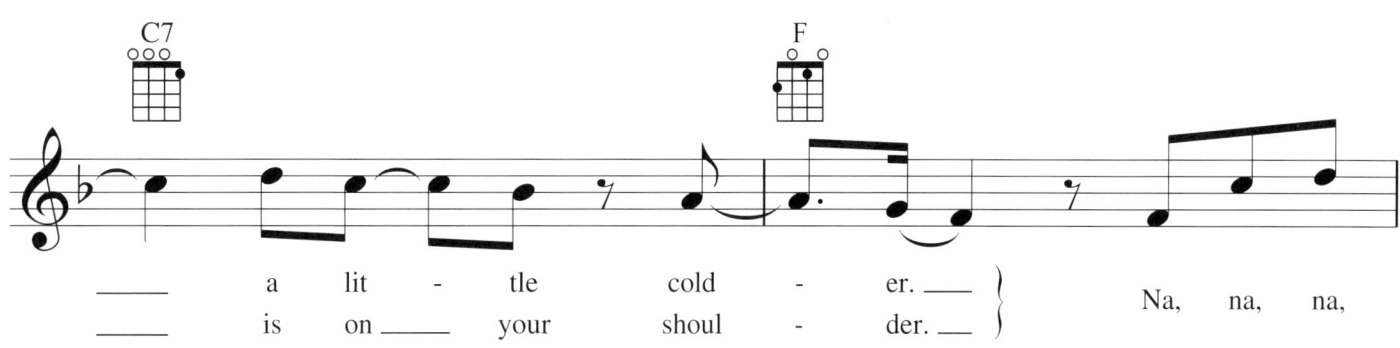

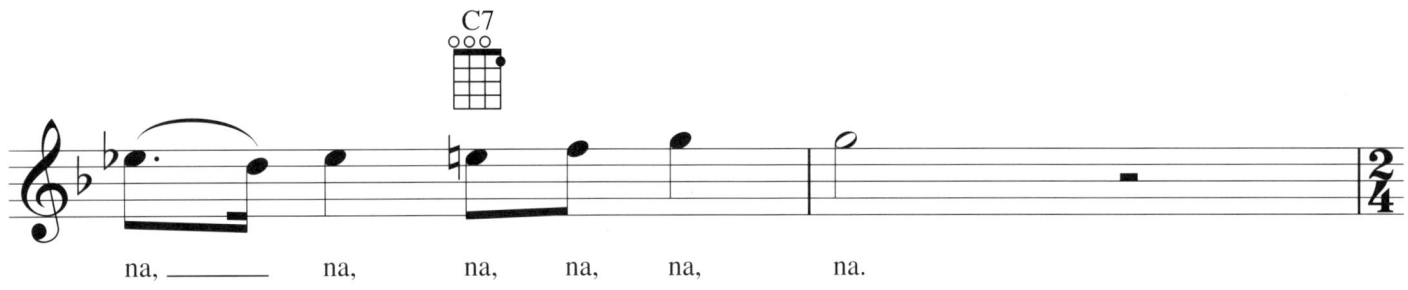
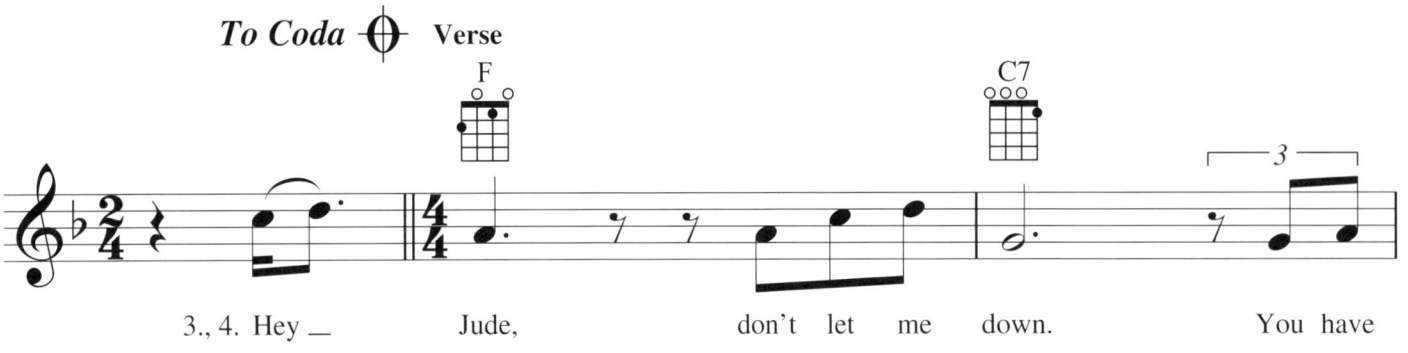

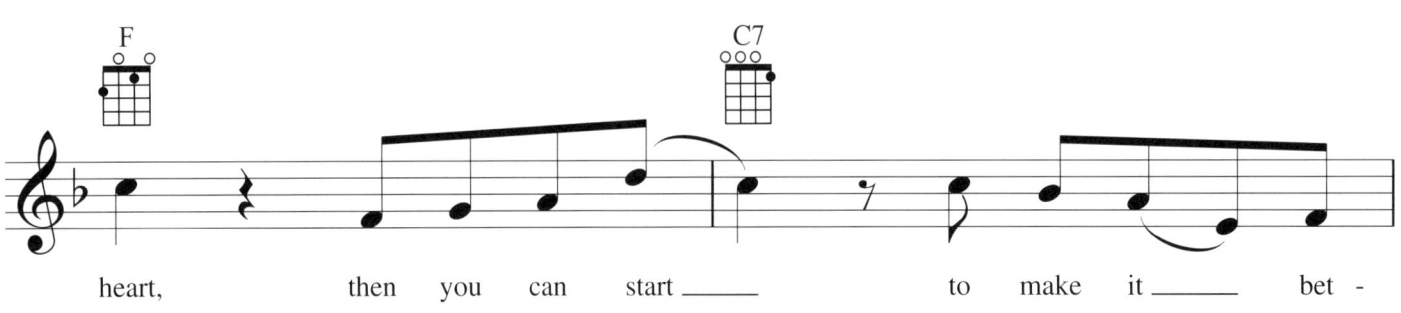
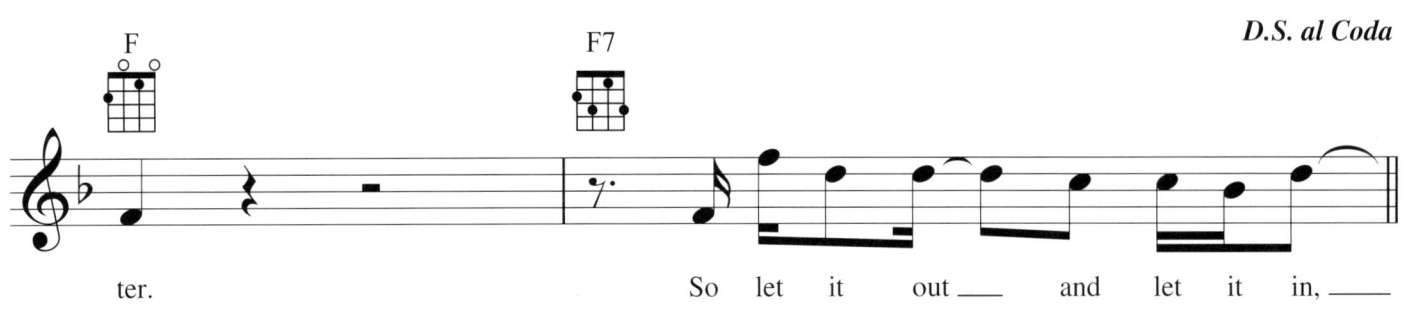

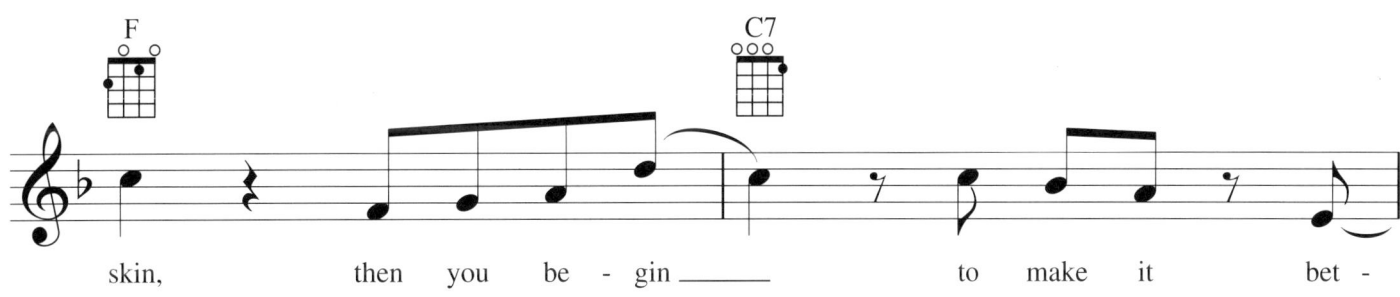
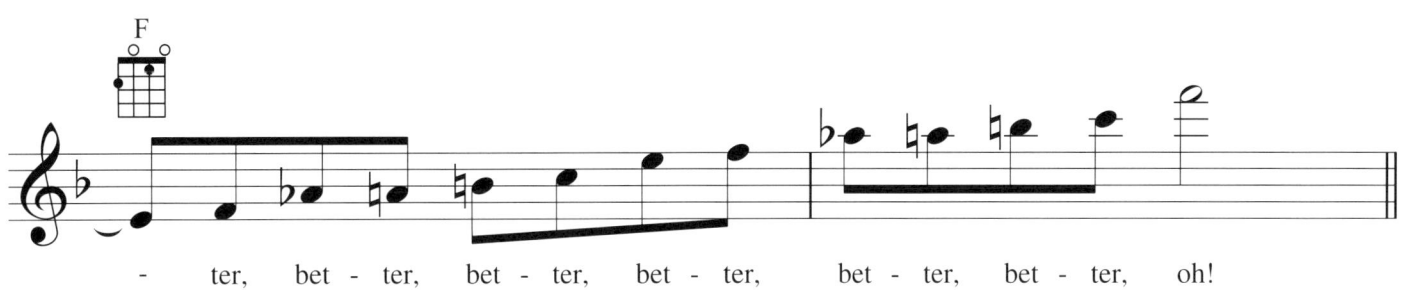
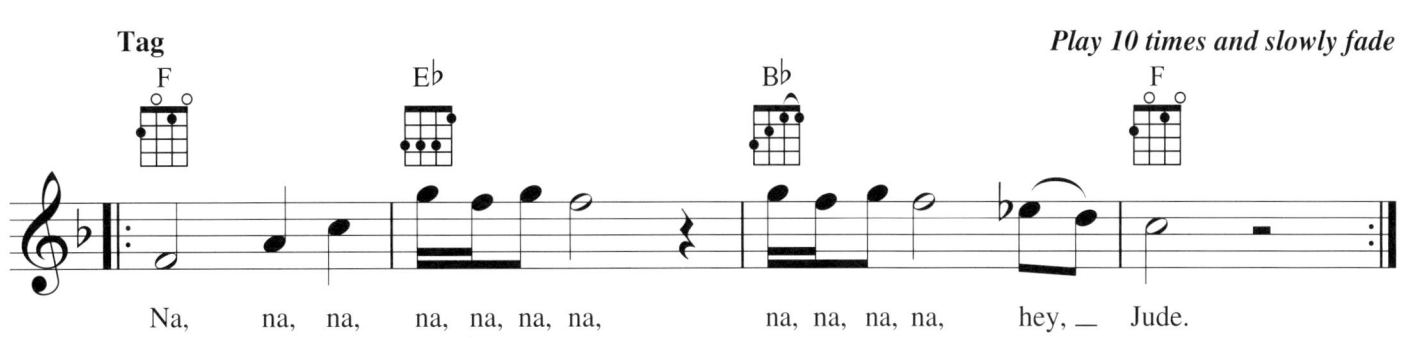

Let It Be

Words and Music by John Lennon and Paul McCartney

TRACK 9

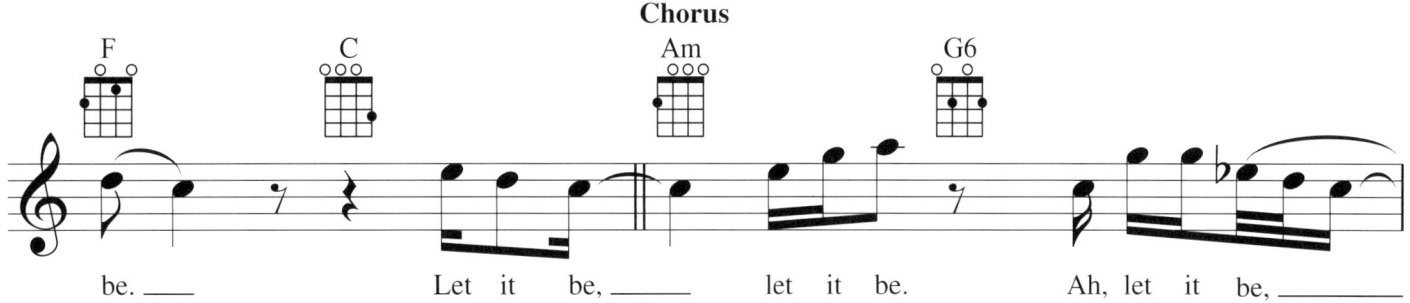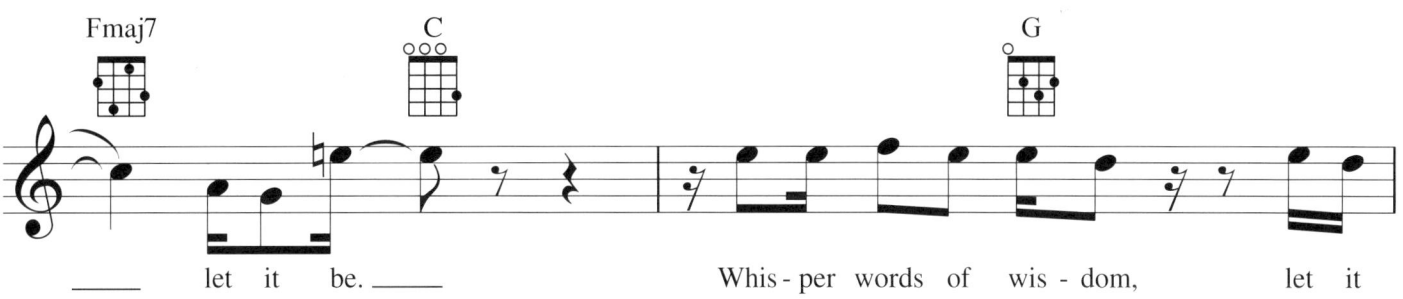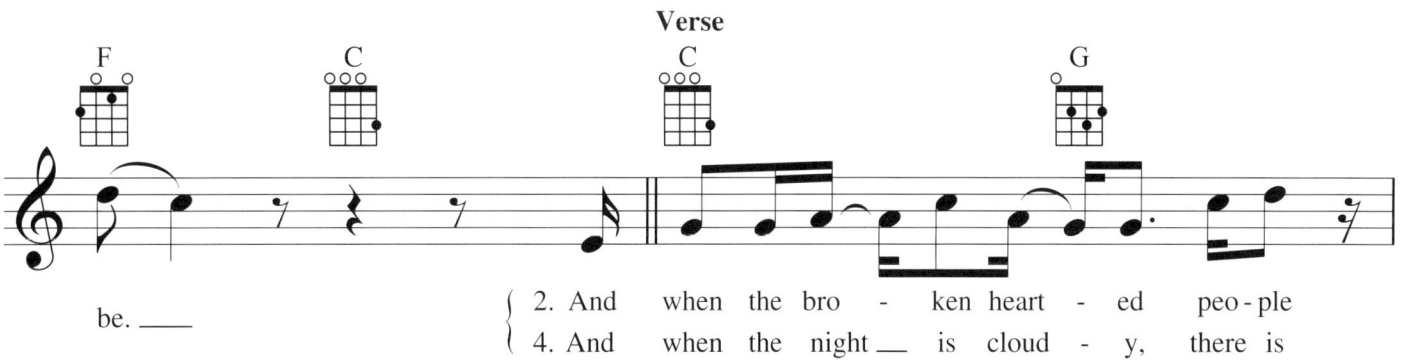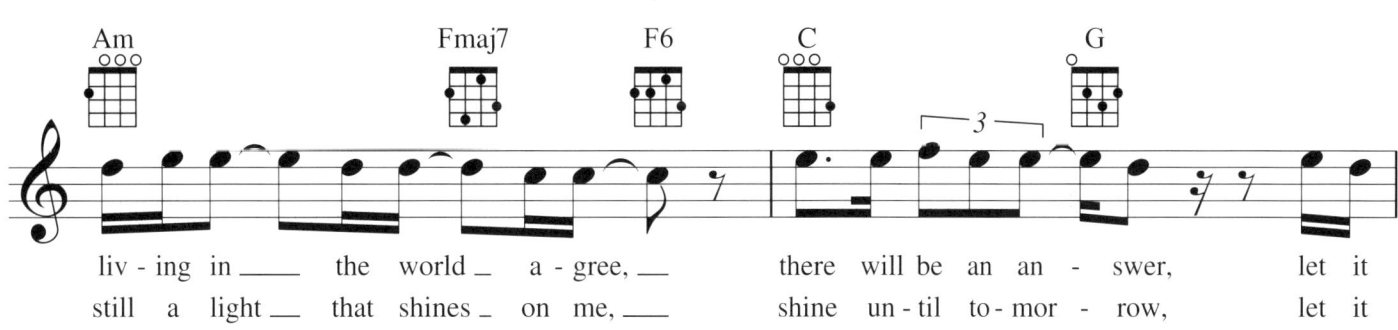

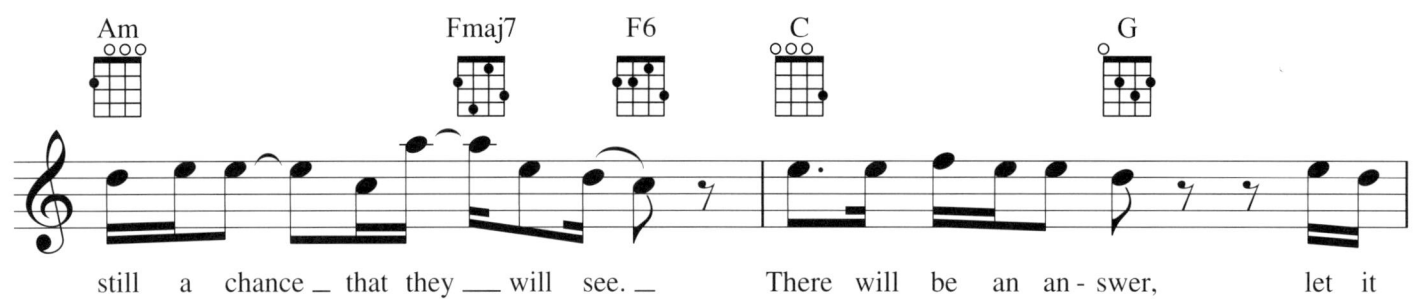
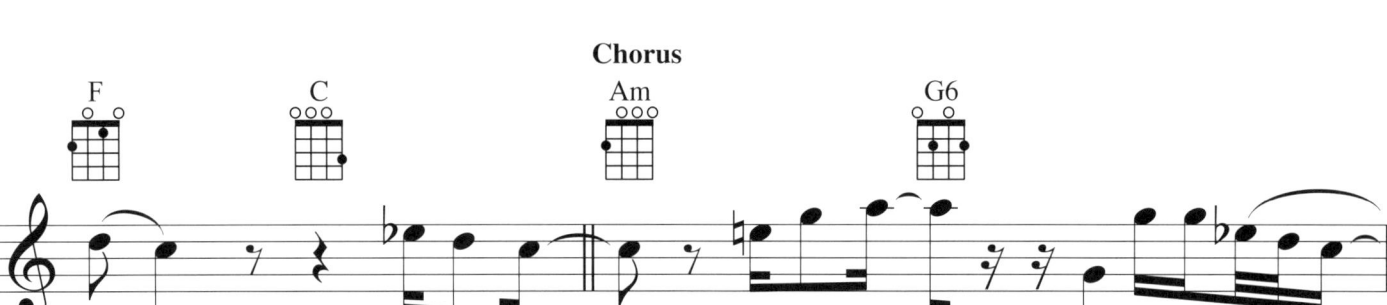

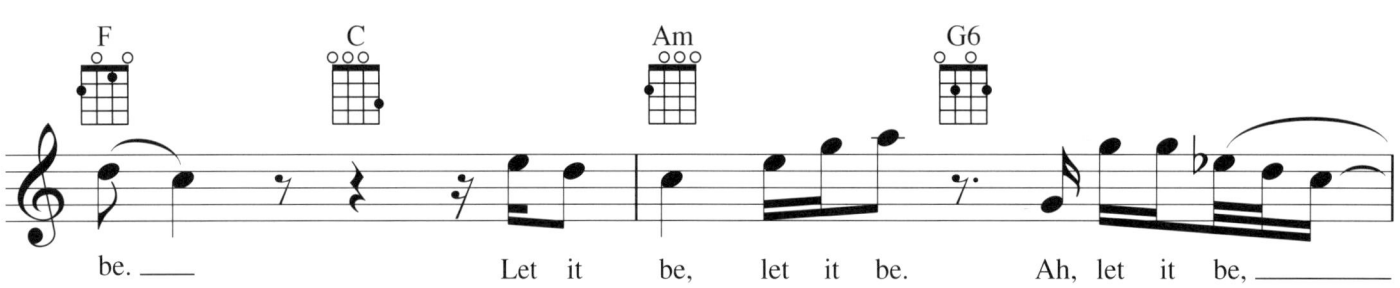
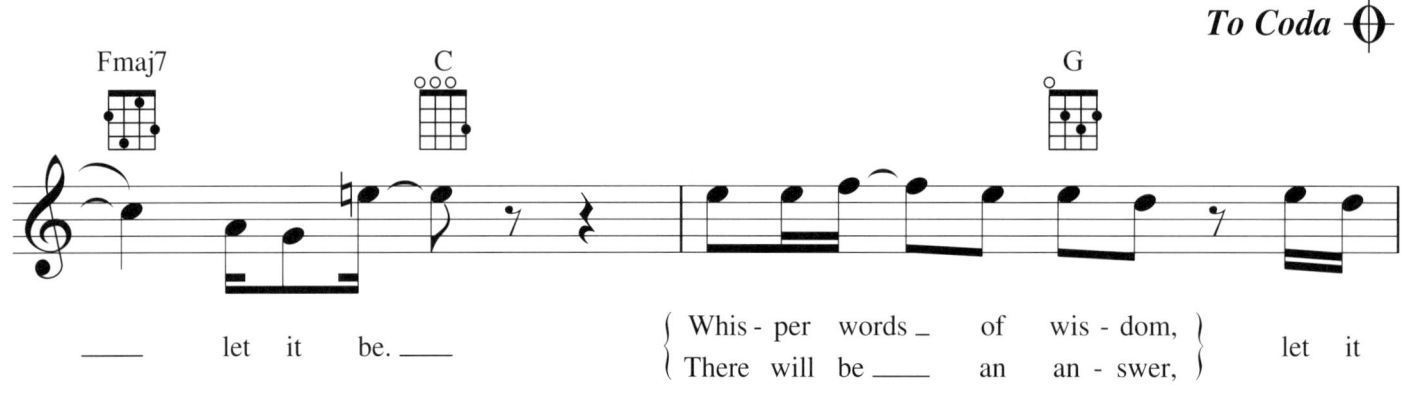

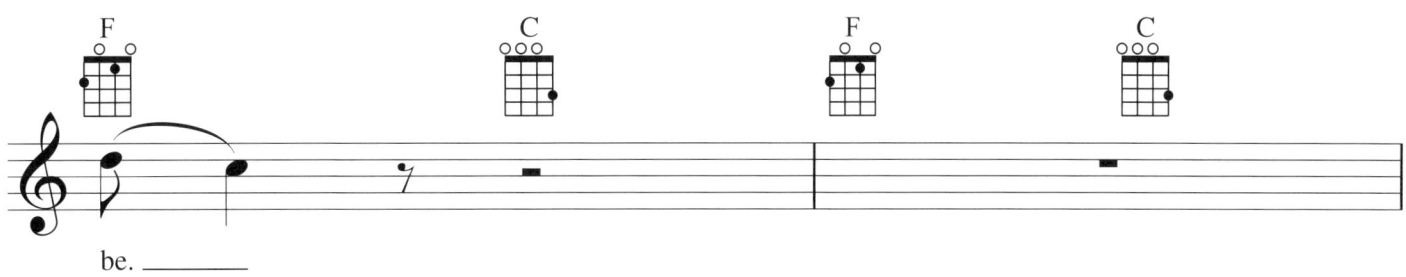
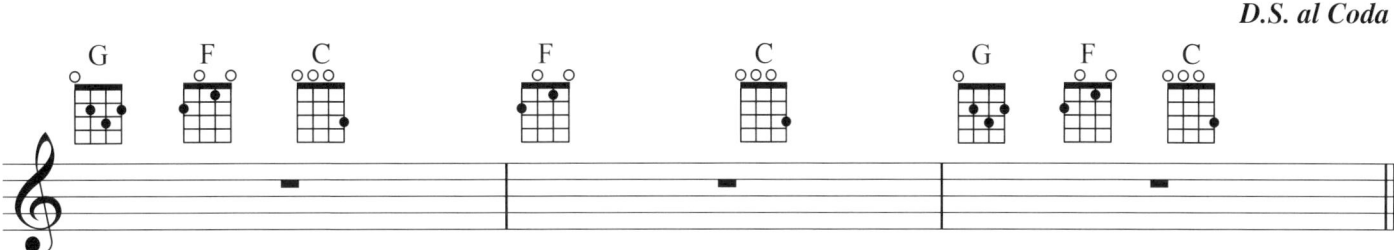
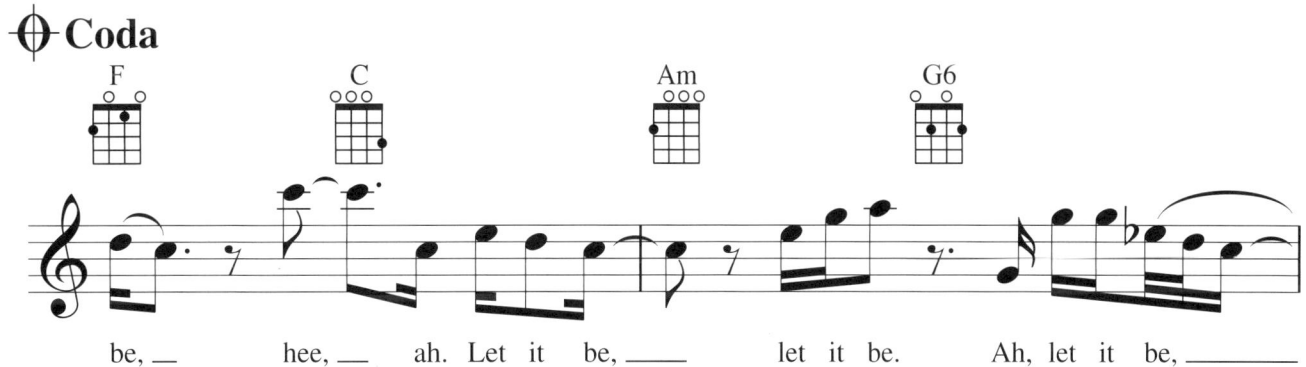
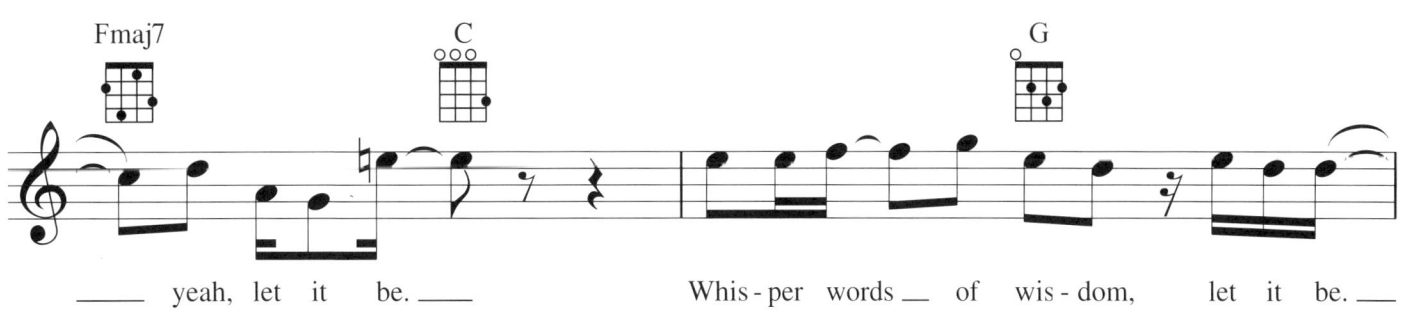
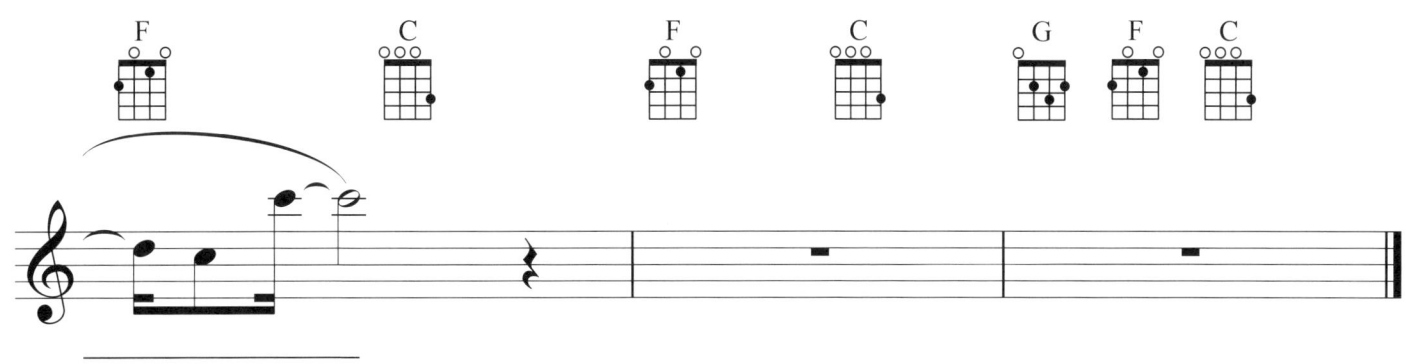

Yesterday

Words and Music by John Lennon and Paul McCartney

TRACK 15

First note

Intro
Moderately ♩ = 98

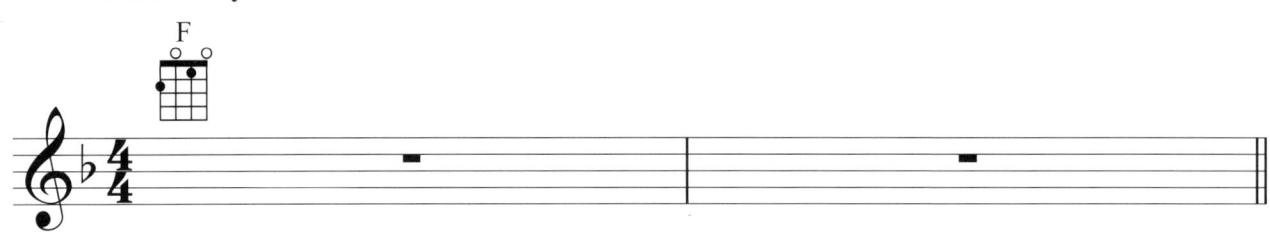

𝄋 Verse

1. Yes-ter-day, all my trou-bles seemed so far a-way.
4. Yes-ter-day, love was such an eas-y game to play.

Now it looks as though they're here to stay.
Now I need a place to hide a-way.

Oh, I be-lieve in

To Coda ⊕ Verse

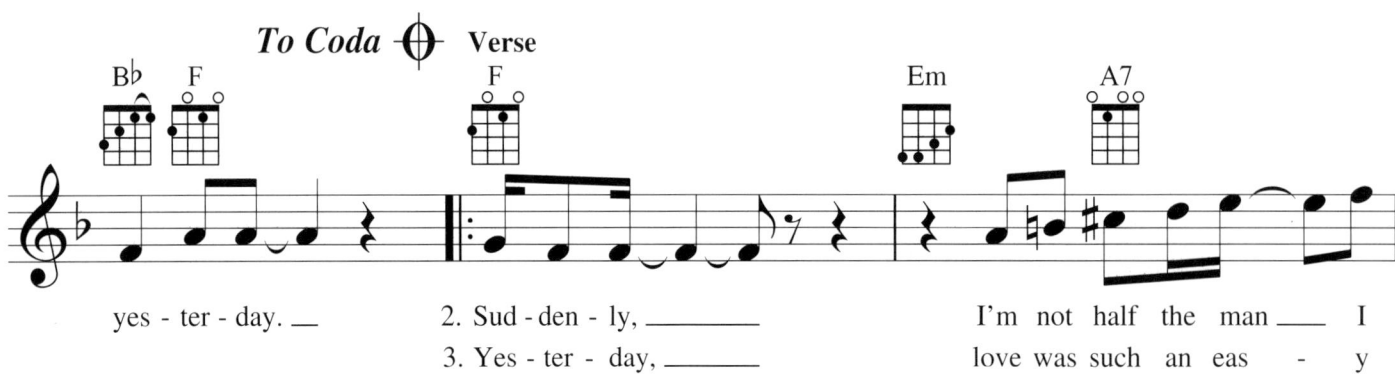

yes-ter-day.

2. Sud-den-ly, I'm not half the man I
3. Yes-ter-day, love was such an eas-y

Nowhere Man

Words and Music by John Lennon and Paul McCartney

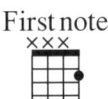
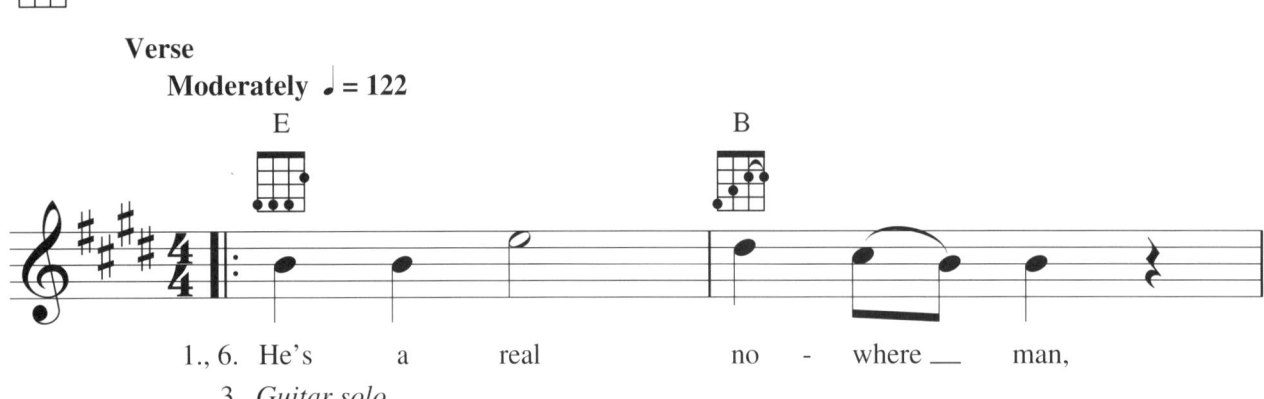

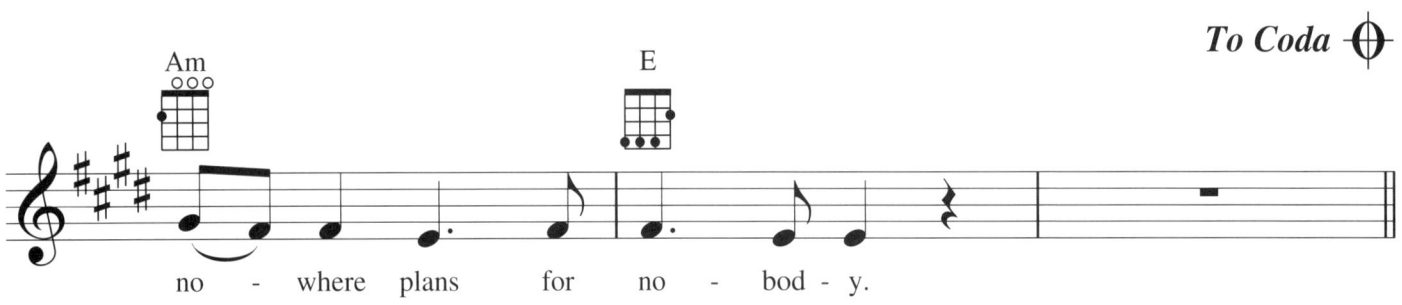
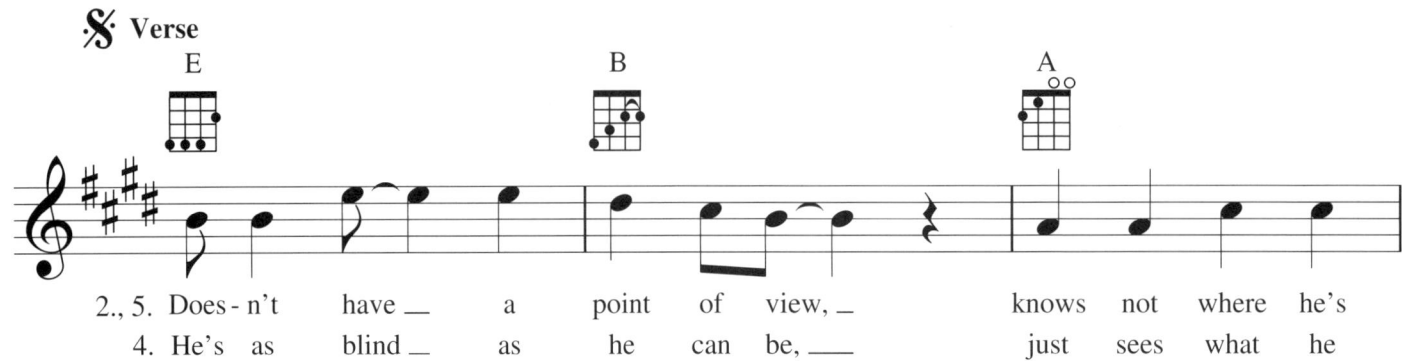

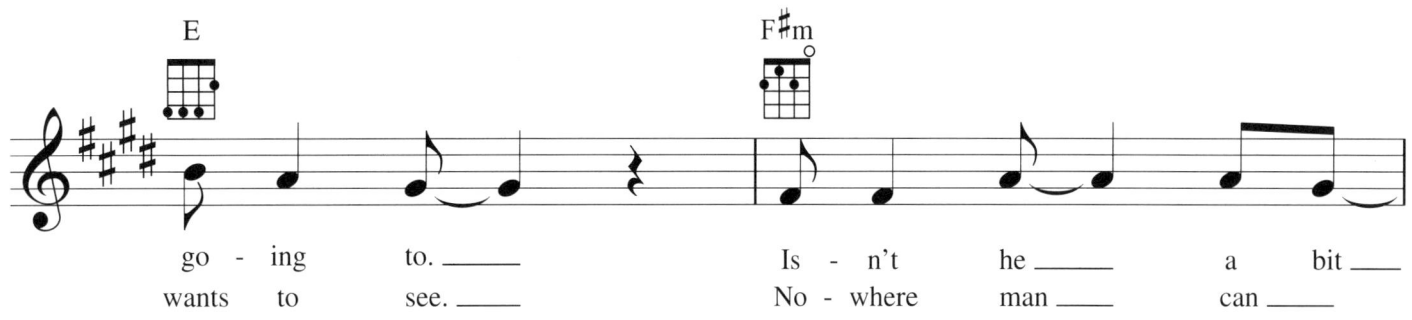

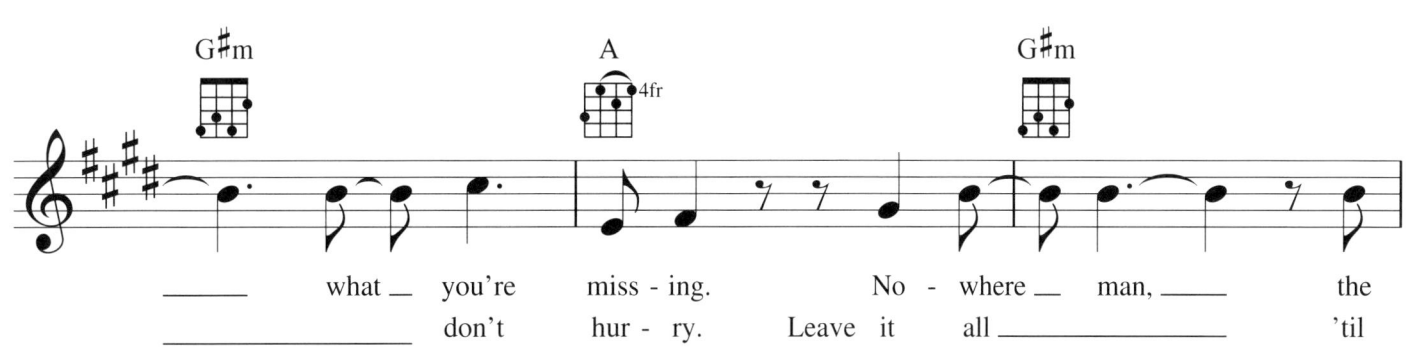

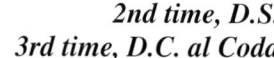

world _____ is at your com - mand.
some - bod - y else ____ lends ___ you a hand. ___

Coda
Tag

Mak - ing all ____ his no - where plans for

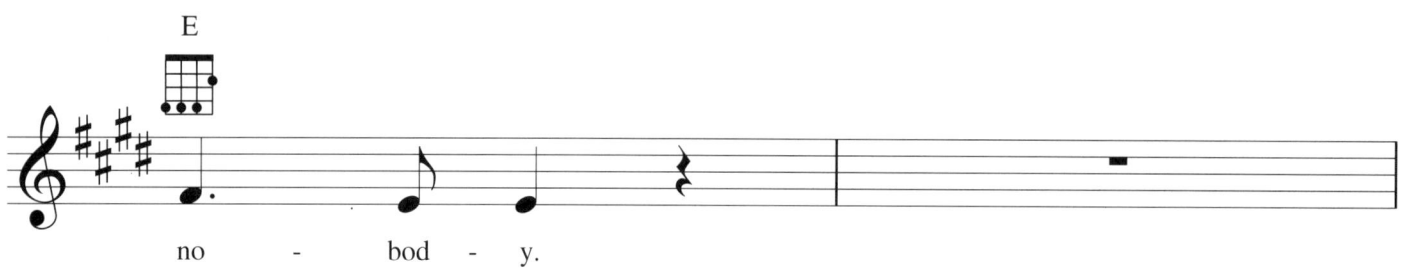

no - bod - y.

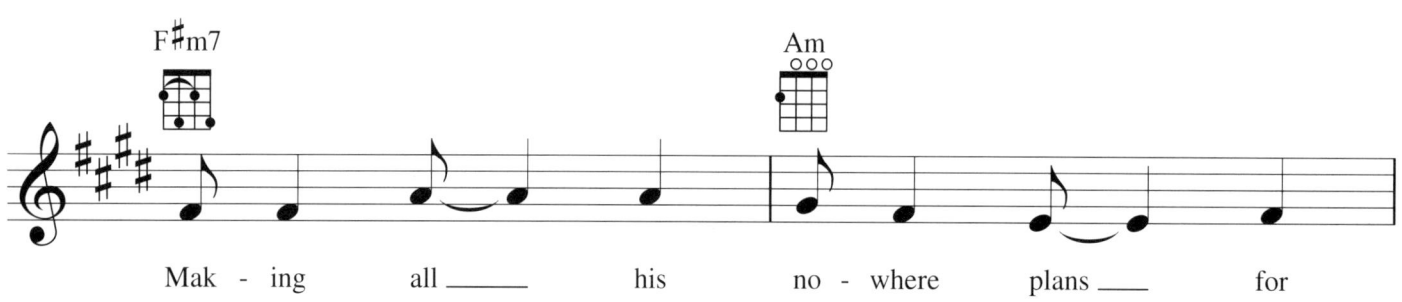

Mak - ing all ____ his no - where plans ___ for

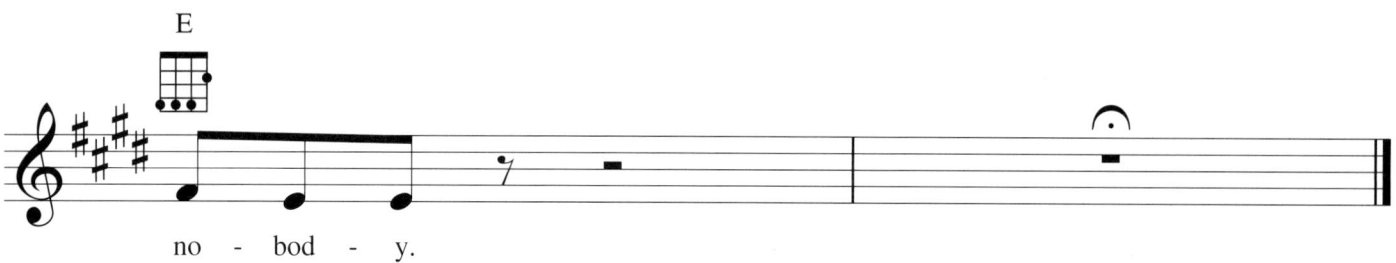

no - bod - y.

Hal Leonard Ukulele Play-Along

AUDIO ACCESS INCLUDED

Now you can play your favorite songs on your uke with great-sounding backing tracks to help you sound like a bona fide pro! The audio also features playback tools so you can adjust the tempo without changing the pitch and loop challenging parts.

1. POP HITS
00701451 Book/CD Pack...............$14.99

2. UKE CLASSICS
00701452 Book/CD Pack...............$12.99

3. HAWAIIAN FAVORITES
00701453 Book/CD Pack...............$12.99

4. CHILDREN'S SONGS
00701454 Book/CD Pack...............$12.99

5. CHRISTMAS SONGS
00701696 Book/CD Pack...............$12.99

6. LENNON & MCCARTNEY
00701723 Book/CD Pack...............$12.99

7. DISNEY FAVORITES
00701724 Book/CD Pack...............$12.99

8. CHART HITS
00701745 Book/CD Pack...............$14.99

9. THE SOUND OF MUSIC
00701784 Book/CD Pack...............$12.99

10. MOTOWN
00701964 Book/CD Pack...............$12.99

11. CHRISTMAS STRUMMING
00702458 Book/CD Pack...............$12.99

12. BLUEGRASS FAVORITES
00702584 Book/CD Pack...............$12.99

13. UKULELE SONGS
00702599 Book/CD Pack...............$12.99

14. JOHNNY CASH
00702615 Book/CD Pack...............$14.99

15. COUNTRY CLASSICS
00702834 Book/CD Pack...............$12.99

16. STANDARDS
00702835 Book/CD Pack...............$12.99

17. POP STANDARDS
00702836 Book/CD Pack...............$12.99

18. IRISH SONGS
00703086 Book/CD Pack...............$12.99

19. BLUES STANDARDS
00703087 Book/CD Pack...............$12.99

20. FOLK POP ROCK
00703088 Book/CD Pack...............$12.99

21. HAWAIIAN CLASSICS
00703097 Book/CD Pack...............$12.99

22. ISLAND SONGS
00703098 Book/CD Pack...............$12.99

23. TAYLOR SWIFT – 2ND EDITION
00221966 Book/Online Audio..........$16.99

24. WINTER WONDERLAND
00101871 Book/CD Pack...............$12.99

25. GREEN DAY
00110398 Book/CD Pack...............$14.99

26. BOB MARLEY
00110399 Book/CD Pack...............$14.99

27. TIN PAN ALLEY
00116358 Book/CD Pack...............$12.99

28. STEVIE WONDER
00116736 Book/CD Pack...............$14.99

29. OVER THE RAINBOW & OTHER FAVORITES
00117076 Book/CD Pack...............$14.99

30. ACOUSTIC SONGS
00122336 Book/CD Pack...............$14.99

31. JASON MRAZ
00124166 Book/CD Pack...............$14.99

32. TOP DOWNLOADS
00127507 Book/CD Pack...............$14.99

33. CLASSICAL THEMES
00127892 Book/Online Audio..........$14.99

34. CHRISTMAS HITS
00128602 Book/CD Pack...............$14.99

35. SONGS FOR BEGINNERS
00129009 Book/Online Audio..........$14.99

36. ELVIS PRESLEY HAWAII
00138199 Book/CD Pack...............$14.99

39. GYPSY JAZZ
00146559 Book/Online Audio..........$14.99

40. TODAY'S HITS
00160845 Book/Online Audio..........$14.99

Prices, contents, and availability subject to change without notice.

HAL•LEONARD®
www.halleonard.com

Ride the Ukulele Wave!

The Beach Boys for Ukulele
This folio features 20 favorites, including: Barbara Ann • Be True to Your School • California Girls • Fun, Fun, Fun • God Only Knows • Good Vibrations • Help Me Rhonda • I Get Around • In My Room • Kokomo • Little Deuce Coupe • Sloop John B • Surfin' U.S.A. • Wouldn't It Be Nice • and more!
00701726 . . . . $14.99

The Beatles for Ukulele
Ukulele players can strum, sing and pick along with 20 Beatles classics! Includes: All You Need Is Love • Eight Days a Week • Good Day Sunshine • Here, There and Everywhere • Let It Be • Love Me Do • Penny Lane • Yesterday • and more.
00700154 . . . . $16.99

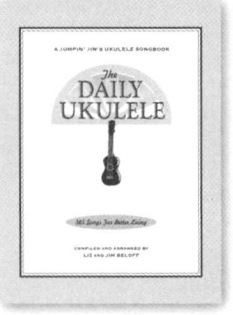

The Daily Ukulele
compiled and arranged by Liz and Jim Beloff
Strum a different song everyday with easy arrangements of 365 of your favorite songs in one big songbook! Includes favorites by the Beatles, Beach Boys, and Bob Dylan, folk songs, pop songs, kids' songs, Christmas carols, and Broadway and Hollywood tunes, all with a spiral binding for ease of use.
00240356 . . . . $39.99

The Daily Ukulele – Leap Year Edition
366 More Songs for Better Living
compiled and arranged by Liz and Jim Beloff
An amazing second volume with 366 MORE songs for you to master each day of a leap year! Includes: Ain't No Sunshine • Calendar Girl • I Got You Babe • Lean on Me • Moondance • and many, many more.
00240681 . . . . $39.99

Disney characters and artwork © Disney Enterprises, Inc.

Disney Songs for Ukulele
20 great Disney classics arranged for all uke players, including: Beauty and the Beast • Bibbidi-Bobbidi-Boo (The Magic Song) • Can You Feel the Love Tonight • Chim Chim Cher-ee • Heigh-Ho • It's a Small World • Some Day My Prince Will Come • We're All in This Together • When You Wish upon a Star • and more.
00701708 . . . . $14.99

First 50 Songs You Should Play on Ukulele
An amazing collection of 50 accessible, must-know favorites: Edelweiss • Hey, Soul Sister • I Walk the Line • I'm Yours • Imagine • Over the Rainbow • Peaceful Easy Feeling • The Rainbow Connection • Riptide • and many more.
00149250 . . . . $14.99

Folk Songs for Ukulele
A great collection to take along to the campfire! 60 folk songs, including: Amazing Grace • Buffalo Gals • Camptown Races • For He's a Jolly Good Fellow • Good Night Ladies • Home on the Range • I've Been Working on the Railroad • Kumbaya • My Bonnie Lies over the Ocean • On Top of Old Smoky • Scarborough Fair • Swing Low, Sweet Chariot • Take Me Out to the Ball Game • Yankee Doodle • and more.
00696068 . . . . $12.99

Hawaiian Songs for Ukulele
Over thirty songs from the state that made the ukulele famous, including: Beyond the Rainbow • Hanalei Moon • Ka-lu-a • Lovely Hula Girl • Mele Kalikimaka • One More Aloha • Sea Breeze • Tiny Bubbles • Waikiki • and more.
00696065 . . . . $10.99

Jack Johnson – Strum & Sing
Cherry Lane Music
Strum along with 41 Jack Johnson songs using this top-notch collection of chords and lyrics just for the uke! Includes: Better Together • Bubble Toes • Cocoon • Do You Remember • Flake • Fortunate Fool • Good People • Holes to Heaven • Taylor • Tomorrow Morning • and more.
02501702 . . . . $15.99

Elvis Presley for Ukulele
arr. Jim Beloff
20 classic hits from The King: All Shook Up • Blue Hawaii • Blue Suede Shoes • Can't Help Falling in Love • Don't • Heartbreak Hotel • Hound Dog • Jailhouse Rock • Love Me • Love Me Tender • Return to Sender • Suspicious Minds • Teddy Bear • and more.
00701004 . . . . $15.99

Jake Shimabukuro – Peace Love Ukulele
Deemed "the Hendrix of the ukulele," Hawaii native Jake Shimabukuro is a uke virtuoso. Our songbook features note-for-note transcriptions with ukulele tablature of Jake's masterful playing on all the CD tracks: Bohemian Rhapsody • Boy Meets Girl • Bring Your Adz • Hallelujah • Pianoforte 2010 • Variation on a Dance 2010 • and more, plus two bonus selections!
00702516 . . . . $19.99

Worship Songs for Ukulele
25 worship songs: Amazing Grace (My Chains are Gone) • Blessed Be Your Name • Enough • God of Wonders • Holy Is the Lord • How Great Is Our God • In Christ Alone • Love the Lord • Mighty to Save • Sing to the King • Step by Step • We Fall Down • and more.
00702546 . . . . $14.99

Prices, contents, and availability subject to change.

Learn to play the Ukulele
with these great Hal Leonard books!

Hal Leonard Ukulele Method Book 1
by Lil' Rev

The *Hal Leonard Ukulele Method* is designed for anyone just learning to play ukulele. This comprehensive and easy-to-use beginner's guide by acclaimed performer and uke master Lil' Rev includes many fun songs of different styles to learn and play. The accompanying CD contains 46 tracks of songs for demonstration and play along. Includes: types of ukuleles, tuning, music reading, melody playing, chords, strumming, scales, tremolo, music notation and tablature, a variety of music styles, ukulele history and much more.

00695847 Book Only.. $5.99
00695832 Book/CD Pack.. $10.99
00320534 DVD... $14.95

Hal Leonard Ukulele Method Book 2
by Lil' Rev

Book 2 picks up where Book 1 left off, featuring more fun songs and examples to strengthen skills and make practicing more enjoyable. Topics include lessons on chord families, hammer-ons, pull-offs, and slides, 6/8 time, ukulele history, and much more. The accompanying CD contains 51 tracks of songs for demonstration and play along.

00695948 Book Only.. $6.99
00695949 Book/CD Pack.. $9.99

Hal Leonard Ukulele Chord Finder
Easy-to-Use Guide to Over 1,000 Ukulele Chords

Learn to play chords on the ukulele with this comprehensive, yet easy-to-use book. *The Ukulele Chord Finder* contains more than a thousand chord diagrams for the most important 28 chord types, including three voicings for each chord. Also includes a lesson on chord construction and a fingerboard chart of the ukulele neck!

00695803 9" x 12"... $6.99
00695902 6" x 9".. $5.99

Hal Leonard Ukulele Scale Finder
by Chad Johnson
Easy-to-Use Guide to Over 1,300 Ukulele Scales

Learn to play scales on the ukulele with this comprehensive yet easy-to-use book. *The Ukulele Scale Finder* contains over 1,300 scale diagrams for the most often-used scales and modes, including multiple patterns for each scale. Also includes a lesson on scale construction and a fingerboard chart of the ukulele neck!

00696378 9" x 12"... $6.99

Easy Songs for Ukulele
Play the Melodies of 20 Pop, Folk, Country, and Blues Songs
by Lil' Rev

Play along with your favorite tunes from the Beatles, Elvis, Johnny Cash, Woody Guthrie, Simon & Garfunkel, and more! The songs are presented in the order of difficulty, beginning with simple rhythms and melodies and ending with chords and notes up the neck. The audio CD features every song played with guitar accompaniment, so you can hear how each song sounds and then play along when you're ready.

00695904 Book/CD Pack.. $14.99
00695905 Book.. $6.99

Irving Berlin Songs Arranged for the "Uke"

20 great songs with full instructions, including: Alexander's Ragtime Band • White Christmas • Easter Parade • Say It with Music • and more.

00005558 7" x 10-1/4"... $6.95

Fretboard Roadmaps – Ukulele
The Essential Patterns That All the Pros Know and Use
by Fred Sokolow & Jim Beloff

Take your uke playing to the next level! Tunes and exercises in standard notation and tab illustrate each technique. Absolute beginners can follow the diagrams and instruction step-by-step, while intermediate and advanced players can use the chapters non-sequentially to increase their understanding of the ukulele. The CD includes 59 demo and play-along tracks.

00695901 Book/CD Pack........................... $14.99

Play Ukulele Today!
A Complete Guide to the Basics
by Barrett Tagliarino

This is the ultimate self-teaching method for ukulele! Includes a CD with full demo tracks and over 60 great songs. You'll learn: care for the instrument; how to produce sound; reading music notation and rhythms; and more.

00699638 Book/CD Pack........................... $9.99

www.halleonard.com

Prices, contents and availability subject to change without notice. Prices listed in U.S. funds.

HAL•LEONARD® CORPORATION
7777 W. BLUEMOUND RD. P.O. BOX 13819
MILWAUKEE, WISCONSIN 53213   0413

Learn To Play Today
with folk music instruction from

Hal Leonard Banjo Method – Second Edition
Authored by Mac Robertson, Robbie Clement & Will Schmid. This innovative method teaches 5-string, bluegrass style. The method consists of two instruction books and two cross-referenced supplement books that offer the beginner a carefully-paced and interest-keeping approach to the bluegrass style.

Method Book 1
00699500 Book $7.99
00695101 Book/CD Pack $16.99

Method Book 2
00699502..$7.99

Supplementary Songbooks
00699515 Easy Banjo Solos......................................$9.99
00699516 More Easy Banjo Solos $9.99

Hal Leonard Dulcimer Method – Second Edition
by Neal Hellman

A beginning method for the Appalachian dulcimer with a unique new approach to solo melody and chord playing. Includes tuning, modes and many beautiful folk songs all demonstrated on the audio accompaniment. Music and tablature.
00699289 Book $8.99
00697230 Book/CD Pack $16.99

The Hal Leonard Complete Harmonica Method – Chromatic Harmonica
by Bobby Joe Holman

The only harmonica method to present the chromatic harmonica in 14 scales and modes in all 12 keys!
00841286 Book/Online Audio..............................$12.99

The Hal Leonard Complete Harmonica Method – The Diatonic Harmonica
by Bobby Joe Holman

This terrific method book/CD pack specific to the diatonic harmonica covers all six positions! It contains more than 20 songs and musical examples.
00841285 Book/CD Pack $12.95

Hal Leonard Fiddle Method
by Chris Wagoner

The Hal Leonard Fiddle Method is the perfect introduction to playing folk, bluegrass and country styles on the violin. Many traditional tunes are included to illustrate a variety of techniques. The accompanying audio includes many tracks for demonstration and play-along. Covers: instrument selection and care; playing positions; theory; slides & slurs; shuffle feel; bowing; drones; playing "backup"; cross-tuning; and much more!
00311415 Book $5.99
00311416 Book/Online Audio................................$9.99

The Hal Leonard Mandolin Method – Second Edition
Noted mandolinist and teacher Rich Del Grosso has authored this excellent mandolin method that features great playable tunes in several styles (bluegrass, country, folk, blues) in standard music notation and tablature. The audio features play-along duets.
00699296 Book $7.99
00695102 Book/Online Audio..............................$15.99

Hal Leonard Oud Method
by John Bilezikjian

This book teaches the fundamentals of standard Western music notation in the context of oud playing. It also covers: types of ouds, tuning the oud, playing position, how to string the oud, scales, chords, arpeggios, tremolo technique, studies and exercises, songs and rhythms from Armenia and the Middle East, and a CD with 25 tracks for demonstration and play along.
00695836 Book/CD Pack $12.99

Hal Leonard Ukulele Method Book 1
by Lil' Rev

This comprehensive and easy-to-use beginner's guide by acclaimed performer and uke master Lil' Rev includes many fun songs of different styles to learn and play. Includes: types of ukuleles, tuning, music reading, melody playing, chords, strumming, scales, tremolo, music notation and tablature, a variety of music styles, ukulele history and much more.
00695847 Book $6.99
00695832 Book/Online Audio..............................$10.99

7777 W. BLUEMOUND RD. P.O. BOX 13819 MILWAUKEE, WI 53213

Visit Hal Leonard Online at
www.halleonard.com